MARTIN LUTHER
IN HIS OWN
WORDS

MARTIN LUTHER
IN HIS OWN
WORDS

Essential Writings of the Reformation

Jack D. Kilcrease
AND
Erwin W. Lutzer, editors

BakerBooks
a division of Baker Publishing Group
Grand Rapids, Michigan

© 2017 by Jack D. Kilcrease and Erwin W. Lutzer

Published by Baker Books
a division of Baker Publishing Group
P.O. Box 6287, Grand Rapids, MI 49516-6287
www.bakerbooks.com

Printed in the United States of America

Library of Congress Cataloging-in-Publication Data is on file at the Library of Congress, Washington, DC.

ISBN 978-0-8010-1932-6 (pbk.)

17 18 19 20 21 22 23   7 6 5 4 3 2 1

Contents

Introduction   7

Sola Fide

1. On Christian Liberty   13
2. Commentary on Galatians: Faith and Works of the Law   33

Sola Gratia

3. Preface to St. Paul's Letter to the Romans   49
4. The Third Article of the Apostles' Creed: The Work of the Holy Spirit   71

Sola Scriptura

5. That Doctrines of Men Are to Be Rejected   83
6. The Bondage of the Will   103

Solus Christus

7. True and False Views of Christ's Suffering   113
8. The Second Article of the Apostles' Creed:
   Jesus Christ   125
9. Commentary on Galatians: Christ Took Our Sin   129

Soli Deo Gloria

10. The First Article of the Apostles' Creed:
    The Gracious God   139
11. The Lord's Prayer   145
12. The First Commandment   159

A Note about Sources   171

INTRODUCTION

Erwin W. Lutzer

This is a book you will want to read more than once.

Dr. Jack D. Kilcrease has given a great gift to the church by collecting these writings and lectures of Martin Luther. He has supplied us with a concise introduction to each reading, updated these classic translations of Luther's writings, and provided footnotes that clarify meaning and explain obscure references that otherwise would be unknown to us. Here we see Luther's passion for those doctrines that lie at the heart of his theology, such as biblical authority, sin, grace, faith, Christ, and the distinction between law and gospel.

Why is it important to read Martin Luther's writings and lectures five hundred years after his lifetime?

The answer is quite simple: his influence is still with us, whether we are Catholic, Protestant, or simply enjoying the freedoms we have come to cherish in the West. Luther stood at a pivotal point in history, between the Dark Ages and the Modern Age, between a time of religious oppression and the growing respect for individual conscience. Standing as he did against one thousand years of religious and political traditions, he planted seeds that continued to grow and benefit us even today.

Let's begin with what Luther was best known for: his rediscovery of the doctrine of justification by faith. This doctrine not only made salvation readily accessible to the average seeker, it also shifted the emphasis away from the church to the individual, and in the process undercut the monopoly that the medieval church had over people's souls. No longer could the pope expect his subjects to obey his official decrees and pronouncements; the people simply did not need his blessing to obtain the salvation that God offered to all who believed. According to Luther, justification meant that God credits sinners with his own righteousness, and this in point of fact is the ground of personal assurance that one has indeed been reborn, fitted for heaven. No wonder he said that this was the doctrine by which the church stands or falls.[1]

Luther also planted the seeds of freedom of religion. In Worms he stood before the emperor and the German princes and boldly declared, "Since then Your Majesty and your lordships desire a simple reply, I will answer without horns and without teeth. . . . My conscience is captive to the Word of God. I cannot and I will not recant anything, for to go against conscience is neither right nor safe. God help me. Amen."[2] When making this clear and simple declaration, he was saying that the conscience of a single monk could challenge the spiritual authority of a thousand years of tradition, the pope, and the powerful grip of the medieval church.

1. In his exposition of Psalm 130:4 Luther wrote, "If this article stands, the church stands; if it falls, the church falls." See Oswald Bayer, *Martin Luther's Theology: A Contemporary Interpretation*, trans. Thomas H. Trapp (Grand Rapids: Eerdmans, 2008), 98n8.
2. Roland Bainton, *Here I Stand—A Life of Martin Luther* (New York: A Mentor Book, 1950), 144.

Luther insisted that belief could not be mandated or coerced. The path to religious freedom in Europe would be fraught with conflict, setbacks, and even wars. But once the idea of freedom of conscience had been introduced, it could not be stopped. After Luther, Europe could not comfortably return to religious suppression and the control of a power-loving church.

Alister McGrath writes, "Luther's doctrine of justification by faith undermined the credibility of the medieval worldview and put in its place something quite different—a way of thinking that placed the relationship between an individual and his or her God at the center of all things. This was an idea that made a powerful appeal in an increasingly individualistic culture."[3]

One of Luther's most enduring legacies is the translating of the Bible into the vernacular and thereby making the Bible available to the common people. Years earlier Guttenberg's printing press had been invented, and now Luther's writings could be spread quickly throughout Europe, eventually followed by Bibles. Luther's Bible not only freed the populace from centuries of tradition but also gave Germany a unified language and a more coherent cultural expression, and it accelerated the spread of the Lutheran faith.

My parents were Germans who grew up in the Ukraine, and they read to us daily from Luther's translation of the German Bible. Like the King James Version in English, Luther's Bible was updated throughout the centuries, but it served as the standard Bible for Germany and other German-speaking countries. If Luther had accomplished only this task, he would have gone down in history as one of the great men of Germany history. That he had so many other accomplishments is a tribute to his genius, courage, and passion.

3. Alister E. McGrath, *Christianity's Dangerous Idea* (New York: HarperCollins, 2007), 45.

Luther believed that the doctrines of the Christian faith should be preached in the language of the people and not in Latin (which few if any of the common people understood). Obviously this exalted the role of the preacher in Protestant congregations. Even in many churches in Europe today, the pulpit, standing as it does above the people, symbolizes that the Word of God is above the congregation. Luther himself preached as regularly as possible when he was home in Wittenberg.

We can neither forget Luther nor ignore him. Even today his writings still constitute a doctrinal divide that has shaped Western Christianity. He wrote and spoke on many topics, such as the relationship of the church and state, Christian marriage, and the growing menace of the Turks who were overrunning parts of Europe. But his greatest contribution had to do with the nature of salvation, the sinfulness of humanity, and the wonder of God's grace.

As you read these pages expect to be blessed and to have your faith strengthened. You will discover that Luther spoke and wrote with deep conviction, wit, and courage. You will better understand his quest for personal salvation and the great discovery he made while teaching the book of Romans: we can neither attain salvation, nor can we contribute to it. Our only contribution is our sin; Jesus supplies the forgiveness and secures our acceptance before our Heavenly Father. Luther said that when he grasped this, he felt as though he was reborn and had entered the gates of Paradise. Imagine his relief when he could say, "My sins belong to Christ as if he had committed them."

Whether or not you agree with every point of Luther's theology, this book is food both for the mind and the soul. Read, contemplate, and give praise to God for the wonder of our redemption. You will discover that for Luther, Christ was always at the center of all things.

SOLA FIDE

1

ON CHRISTIAN LIBERTY

Luther's treatise *On Christian Liberty* (1520) was written in the wake of several significant events, including the Leipzig debate, his excommunication by Pope Leo X, and very probably his so-called Reformation breakthrough. Luther's main purpose in this treatise was to explain his new understanding of the justification of the sinner before God.

Luther begins the treatise by telling his readers that the Christian is a "free lord of all and subject to none; a Christian is the most dutiful servant of all and subject to everyone." Luther explicates the first part of this description ("free lord of all and subject to none") by noting that it describes only the believer's inner person before the eyes of God. The second statement applies to the external person as the believer exists and acts before the eyes of the world.

Throughout this treatise, Luther often uses the language of "spirit" and "flesh." This may confuse many readers into thinking that Luther is speaking of a mind/body dualism not dissimilar to Greek philosophy or some East Asian religions. But this would be a misinterpretation. Rather, Luther merely wishes to distinguish between one's inner person (spirit) whose conscience stands before the judgment seat of

God, and the external person who relates to other human beings and the created world in general through the medium of the body.

Luther tells his readers that in order to receive justifying faith they must first be humbled through the condemnation brought by God's commandments. Although God does give us commandments as a means to guide our lives, according to Luther, this is only a secondary function of the law. Primarily, God has given his law as a means of revealing human sin. The revelation of sin necessarily humbles people into recognizing that they need God's gift of salvation in Jesus.

Faith is created through the preaching of the promise of the gospel only after God has worked repentance through the preaching of the law. By faith, the believer receives the fullness of Christ's righteousness through the Word. In the gospel promise, Christ utterly surrenders himself to the believer. Just as there is an exchange of assets and property between a man and woman when they get married, so too there is an exchange of realities between Christ and the believer. Christ gives the believer his life and righteousness, whereas the believer gives Christ his or her personal sin and death.

Faith therefore gives the believer a share in Christ's infinite riches of righteousness, life, and dominion. Because Christians share Christ's riches, they are therefore free to give of these riches to their neighbors. God does not need our good works, since all has been paid for by Christ. Instead, the neighbor needs the believer's good works. The believer obeys God and gives the neighbor a share in the riches of Christ through the good works of loving service.

The following is a selection from the treatise.

I first lay down these two propositions, concerning spiritual liberty and servitude. A Christian is the free lord of all and subject to none; a Christian is the most dutiful servant of all and subject to everyone.

Although these statements appear contradictory, yet when the agreement between them is seen, they will be highly useful to my purpose. They are both the statements of Paul himself, who says, "For though I am free from all, I have made myself a servant to all" (1 Cor. 9:19), and "Owe no one anything, except to love each other" (Rom. 13:8). Now love is by its own nature dutiful and obedient to the object that it loves. Thus even Christ, though Lord of all things, was yet born of a woman, placed under the law, at once free and a servant, at once in the form of God and in the form of a servant.

Let us examine the subject on a deeper and less simple principle. Man[1] is composed of a twofold nature, one spiritual and the other bodily. Regarding the spiritual nature, which is named the soul, he is called the spiritual, inward, new man. As regards the bodily nature, which is named the flesh, he is called the fleshly, outward, old man. The apostle speaks of this: "Though our outer self is wasting away, our inner self is being renewed day by day" (2 Cor. 4:16). The result of this diversity is that in the Scriptures opposing statements are made concerning the same man; the fact being that in the same man these two men are opposed to one another; the flesh lusting against the spirit, and the spirit against the flesh (Gal. 5:17).

First, let us consider the inward man so as to see by what means a man becomes justified, free, and a true Christian—that is, a spiritual, new, and inward man. It is certain that nothing outward, under whatever name they may be called, has any ability in producing a state of justification and Christian liberty or, on the other hand, unrighteousness and one of slavery. A simple argument will prove this statement.

What can it profit the soul that the body should be in good condition, free, and full of life, that it should eat, drink, and

1. The masculine generic "man" and "men" have generally been retained in the translations throughout, reflecting Luther's original writing.

do what it wishes? For in these respects even impious slaves of every kind of vice can prosper. Again, what harm can ill health, bondage, hunger, thirst, or any other outward evil do to the soul when even the most pious of men, and the freest in the purity of their conscience, are afflicted by these things? Neither of these states of things has to do with the liberty or the slavery of the soul.

And so it will not profit the body if it is adorned with sacred vestments, or dwells in holy places, or is occupied in sacred offices,[2] or prays, fasts, and abstains from certain meats, or does whatever works can be done through the body and in the body. Something widely different will be necessary for the justification and liberty of the soul, since the things I have spoken of can be done by any impious person and only hypocrites are produced by devotion to these things. On the other hand, it will not at all injure the soul that the body should wear profane clothing, should dwell in profane places, should eat and drink in the ordinary fashion, should not pray aloud, and should leave undone all the aforementioned things, which may be done by hypocrites.

And, to cast everything aside, even speculations, meditations, and whatever things can be performed by the exertions of the soul itself are of no profit. But one thing is necessary for life, justification, and Christian liberty. That is the most holy Word of God, the gospel of Christ, as he says, "I am the resurrection and the life. Whoever believes in me, though he die, yet shall he live" (John 11:25); and also, "If the Son sets you free, you will be free indeed" (John 8:36); and, "Man shall not live by bread alone, but by every word that comes from the mouth of God" (Matt. 4:4).

2. "Sacred offices" would be the offices of the priesthood, or possibly even monastic offices. In medieval Catholicism monks and the clergy were considered higher in the hierarchy of human society than ordinary Christians.

Let us therefore hold to be firmly established that the soul can do without everything except the Word of God, without which none at all of its wants are provided for. But, having the Word, it is rich and lacks nothing, since that is the Word of life, truth, light, peace, justification, salvation, joy, liberty, wisdom, virtue, grace, glory, and all good things. It is on this account that the prophet in a whole psalm (Ps. 119) and in many other places sighs for and calls on the Word of God with so many groans and words.

Again, there is no crueler blow of the wrath of God than when he sends a famine of hearing his words (Amos 8:11). Likewise, there is no greater favor from him than the sending forth of his Word, as it is said, "He sent out his word and healed them, and delivered them from their destruction" (Ps. 107:20). Christ was sent for no other office than that of the Word, and the order of apostles, that of bishops, and that of the whole body of the clergy have been called and instituted for no object but the ministry of the Word.

But you will ask, "What is this Word, and by what means is it to be used, since there are so many words of God?" I answer, the apostle Paul (Rom. 1) explains what it is—namely, the gospel of God, concerning his Son, incarnate, suffering, risen, and glorified through the Spirit, the sanctifier. To preach Christ is to feed the soul, to justify it, to set it free, and to save it, if it believes the preaching. For faith alone, and the efficacious use of the Word of God, brings salvation. "If you confess with your mouth that Jesus is Lord and believe in your heart that God raised him from the dead, you will be saved" (Rom. 10:9). And again, "For Christ is the end of the law for righteousness to everyone who believes" (Rom. 10:4); and, "The righteous shall live by faith" (Rom. 1:17). For the Word of God cannot be received and honored by any works, but by faith alone. Hence it is clear that as the soul needs the Word alone for life and justification, so it is justified by faith alone and not by any works. For if it could be justified by any other means, it would have no need of the Word, nor consequently of faith.

But this faith cannot consist at all with works—that is, if you imagine that you can be justified by those works, whatever their character. For this would be to stand between two opinions, to worship Baal and to kiss one's own hand, which is a great sin, as Job says [Job 31:27]. Therefore, when you begin to believe, you learn at the same time that all that is in you is utterly guilty, sinful, and damnable, as according to that saying: "All have sinned and fall short of the glory of God" (Rom. 3:23). And also, "None is righteous, no, not one; no one understands; no one seeks for God. All have turned aside; together they have become worthless; no one does good, not even one" (Rom. 3:10–12). When you have learned this, you will know that Christ is necessary for you, since he has suffered and risen again for you, that, believing on him, you might by this faith become another man, all your sins being remitted, and you being justified by the merits of another—namely, of Christ alone.

Since then this faith can reign only in the inward man, as it is said, "For with the heart one believes and is justified" (Rom. 10:10); and since it alone justifies, it is evident that by no outward work or labor can the inward man be at all justified, made free, and saved, and that no works whatever have any relation to him. And so, on the other hand, it is solely by impiety and unbelief of heart that he becomes guilty and a slave of sin, deserving damnation, not by any outward sin or work. Therefore the first care of every Christian ought to be to lay aside all reliance on works, strengthen his faith alone more and more, and by it grow in the knowledge not of works but of Christ Jesus, who has suffered and risen again for him, as Peter teaches, when he makes no other work [but faith] to be a Christian one. Thus Christ, when the Jews asked him what they should do that they might work the works of God, rejected the multitude of works, with which he saw that they were puffed up, and commanded them one thing only, saying, "This is the work of God, that you believe in him whom he has sent" (John 6:29). "For on him God the Father has set his seal" (John 6:27). . . .

. . . Meanwhile it is to be noted that the whole Scripture of God is divided into two parts, commandments and promises. The commandments certainly teach us what is good, but they cannot be done immediately when they are taught. For they show us what we ought to do but do not give us the power to do it. They were ordained, however, for the purpose of showing man to himself, that through them he may learn his own inability to do the good and may despair of his own strength. For this reason they are called the Old Testament and are so.[3]

For example, "Do not covet" is a commandment by which we are all convicted of sin, since no man can help coveting, whatever efforts to the contrary he may make. In order, therefore, that he may fulfill the commandment and not covet, he is driven to despair in himself and to seek elsewhere and through another the help that he cannot find in himself; as it is said, "O Israel, for you are against me, against your helper" (Hos. 13:9). Now what is done by this one commandment is done by them all. For all [commandments] are equally impossible for us to fulfill.

Now, when a man through the commandments has been taught his own impotence and becomes anxious by what means

3. By "Old Testament" Luther does not here mean that everything in the books of the Old Testament are identical with the law of God. Neither does he mean that everything in the New Testament books is a promise of God's grace. Rather, he means that there is an "Old Covenant" (or "Testament"), the Sinaitic covenant that demands, and a "New Covenant" (or "Testament"), the promise of grace for the sake of Christ. Both covenants are present in the whole of the Bible.

he may satisfy the law (for the law must be satisfied, so that no jot or tittle of it may pass away, otherwise he must be hopelessly condemned), then, being truly humbled and brought to nothing in his own eyes, he finds in himself no resource for justification and salvation. Then comes in that other part of Scripture, the promises of God, which declare the glory of God and say, "If you wish to fulfill the law, and, as the law requires, not to covet, believe in Christ, in whom are promised to you grace, justification, peace, and liberty." All these things you shall have if you believe, and shall be without them if you do not believe. For what is impossible for you by all the works of the law, which are many and yet useless, you shall fulfill in an easy and summary way through faith. Indeed, God the Father has made everything to depend on faith, so that whosoever has it has all things and he who has it not has nothing: "For God has consigned all to disobedience, that he may have mercy on all" (Rom. 11:32).

Thus the promises of God give that which the commandments demand and fulfill what the law commands, so that all is of God alone, both the precepts and their fulfillment. He alone commands. He alone also fulfills. Therefore, the promises of God belong to the New Testament. Indeed, they are the New Testament.

Now since these promises of God are words of holiness, truth, righteousness, liberty, and peace and are full of universal goodness, the soul that cleaves to them with a firm faith is so united to them, indeed, so thoroughly absorbed by them, that it not only partakes in but is penetrated and saturated by all their virtue. For if the touch of Christ was healing, how much more [does] that tender spiritual touch, indeed, absorption of the Word, communicate to the soul all that belongs to the Word? In this way, therefore, the soul, through faith alone, without works, is from the Word of God justified, sanctified, endued with truth, peace, and liberty, and filled full with every good thing and is truly made the child of God. As it is said: "But to all who did receive him, who believed in his name, he gave the right to become children of God" (John 1:12).

From all this it is easy to understand why faith has such great power and why no good works, nor even all good works put together, can compare with it, since no work can cleave to the Word of God or be in the soul. Faith alone and the Word reign in it. And such as is the Word, such is the soul made by it, just as iron exposed to fire glows like fire on account of its union with the fire. It is clear then that for a Christian his faith suffices for everything and that he has no need of works for justification. But if he has no need of works, neither does he have any need of the law, and if he has no need of the law, he is certainly free from the law, and the saying is true: "The law is not laid down for the just" (1 Tim. 1:9). This is that Christian liberty, our faith, the effect of which is not that we should be careless or lead a bad life but that no one should need the law or works for justification and salvation.

. . . The third incomparable grace of faith is this, that it unites the soul to Christ, as the wife to the husband, by which mystery, as the apostle teaches, Christ and the soul are made one flesh. Now if they are one flesh, and if a true marriage—indeed, by far the most perfect of all marriages is accomplished between them (for human marriages are but poor types of this one great marriage)—then it follows that they hold all in common, good things as well as bad things. Likewise, whatsoever Christ possesses, the believing soul may take to itself and boast of as its own, and whatever belongs to the soul, Christ claims as his.

If we compare these possessions, we will see how inestimable the gain is: Christ is full of grace, life, and salvation; the soul is full of sin, death, and condemnation. Let faith step in, and then sin, death, and hell will belong to Christ, and grace, life, and salvation to the soul. For, if he is a husband, he must necessarily take on himself that which is his wife's and, at the same time, give to his wife that which is his. For in giving her his own body and himself, how can he but give her all that is his? And in taking to himself the body of his wife, how can he but take to himself all that is hers?

In this is displayed the delightful sight, not only of communion but of a prosperous warfare, of victory, salvation, and redemption. Christ is God and man in one person, and as neither has sinned, nor dies, nor is condemned—indeed, cannot sin, die, or be condemned—and since his righteousness, life, and salvation are invincible, eternal, and almighty, therefore I say that when such a person, by the wedding ring of faith, takes a share in the sins, death, and hell of his wife—indeed, makes them his own—and deals with them in no other way than as if they were his and as if he himself had sinned; and when he suffers, dies, and descends to hell, that he may overcome all things, since sin, death, and hell cannot swallow him up, they must be swallowed up by him in stupendous conflict. For his righteousness rises above the sins of all men, his life is more powerful than all death, and his salvation is more unconquerable than all hell.

Thus the believing soul, by the pledge of its faith in Christ, becomes free from all sin, fearless of death, safe from hell, and endowed with the eternal righteousness, life, and salvation of its husband, Christ. Thus he presents to himself a glorious bride, without spot or wrinkle, cleansing her with the washing of water by the Word—that is, by faith in the Word of life, righteousness, and salvation. Thus he betroths her to himself "in righteousness and in justice, in steadfast love and in mercy" (Hos. 2:19).

Who then can value this royal marriage highly enough? Who can comprehend the riches of the glory of this grace? Christ, that rich and pious husband, takes as a wife a needy and impious prostitute, redeeming her from all her evils and supplying her with all his good things. It is impossible now that her sins should destroy her, since they have been laid on Christ and swallowed up in him, and since she has in her husband, Christ, a righteousness that she may claim as her own and that she can set up with confidence against all her sins, against death and hell, saying, "If I have sinned, my Christ, in whom I believe, has not sinned; all mine is his, and all his is mine," as it is written, "My beloved is mine, and I am his" (Song 2:16). This is what Paul says: "Thanks be to God, who gives us the victory through our Lord Jesus Christ"—victory over sin and death, as he says: "The sting of death is sin, and the power of sin is the law" (1 Cor. 15:57, 56).

From all this you will again understand why so much importance is attributed to faith, so that it alone can fulfill the law and justify without any works. For you see that the first commandment, which says, "You shall worship one God only," is fulfilled by faith alone. If you were nothing but good works from the soles of your feet to the crown of your head, you would not be worshiping God nor fulfilling the first commandment, since it is impossible to worship God without ascribing to him the glory of truth and of universal goodness, as it ought in truth to be ascribed. Now this is not done by works but only by faith of heart. It is not by working but by believing that we glorify God and confess him to be true. On this ground faith is the sole righteousness of a Christian man and the fulfilling of all the commandments. For to him who fulfills the first, the task of fulfilling all the rest is easy.

Works, since they are irrational things, cannot glorify God, although they may be done to the glory of God if faith is present. But at present we are inquiring not into the quality of the works done but into him who does them, who glorifies God and brings forth good works. This is faith of heart, the head and the substance of all our righteousness. Hence that is a blind and dangerous doctrine which teaches that the commandments are fulfilled by works. The commandments must have been fulfilled previous to any good works, and good works follow their fulfillment, as we shall see.

But that we may have a wider view of that grace which our inner man has in Christ, we must know that in the Old Testament God sanctified to himself every firstborn male. The birthright was of great value, giving a superiority over the rest by the double honor of priesthood and kingship. For the firstborn brother was priest and lord of all the rest.

Under this figure was foreshown Christ, the true and only firstborn of God the Father and of the Virgin Mary, and a true king and priest, not in a fleshly and earthly sense. For his kingdom is not of this world. It is in heavenly and spiritual things that he reigns and acts as priest; and these are righteousness, truth, wisdom, peace, salvation, etc. All things, even those of earth and hell, are subject to him, for otherwise how could he defend and save us from them? But it is not in these, nor by these, that his kingdom stands.

So too his priesthood does not consist in the outward display of priestly clothing and gestures, as did the human priesthood of Aaron and our contemporary ecclesiastical priesthood, but in spiritual things, wherein in his invisible office he intercedes for us with God in heaven and there offers himself and performs all the duties of a priest, as Paul[4] describes him to the Hebrews

---

4. Later in life Luther came to doubt Paul's authorship of the Letter to the Hebrews (today Hebrews is almost universally held to have been written by someone other than Paul). But here he assumes, with most other medieval interpreters, that it was written by Paul.

under the figure of Melchizedek. Nor does he only pray and
intercede for us; he also teaches us inwardly in the spirit with
the living teachings of his Spirit. Now those are the two special
offices of a priest, as is figured to us in the case of fleshly priests,
by visible prayers and sermons.

As Christ by his birthright has obtained these two dignities,
so he imparts and communicates them to every believer in him,
under that law of matrimony of which we have spoken above
by which all that is the husband's is also the wife's. Hence all
we who believe on Christ are kings and priests in Christ, as it
is said: "But you are a chosen race, a royal priesthood, a holy
nation, a people for his own possession, that you may proclaim
the excellences of him who called you out of darkness into his
marvelous light" (1 Pet. 2:9).

These two things are related like this: First, as regards kingship, every Christian is by faith so exalted above all things that, in
spiritual power, he is completely lord of all things, so that nothing
can hurt him; all things are subject to him and are compelled to
be subservient to his salvation. Thus Paul says, "We know that
for those who love God all things work together for good, for
those who are called according to his purpose" (Rom. 8:28); and
also, "The world or life or death or the present or the future—all
are yours, and you are Christ's" (1 Cor. 3:22–23). It is not in the
sense of earthly power that Christians possess and rule all things,
contrary to the insane and senseless idea of certain church officials. That is the office of kings, princes, and men on earth. In the
experience of life we see that we are subjected to all things and
suffer many things, even death. Indeed, the more of a Christian
any man is, he is subjected to more evils, sufferings, and deaths,
as we see in Christ the firstborn and in all his holy brothers.

This is a spiritual power that rules in the midst of enemies
and is powerful in the midst of distress. And this is nothing else

than that strength is made perfect in my weakness and that I can turn all things to the profit of my salvation so that even the cross and death are compelled to serve me and to work together for my salvation. This is a lofty and eminent dignity, a true and almighty dominion, a spiritual empire, in which there is nothing so good, nothing so bad, that it does not work together for my good if only I believe. And yet there is nothing I need. For faith alone suffices for my salvation. Faith may exercise the power and empire of its freedom. This is the inestimable power and freedom of Christians.

We are not only the freest of all kings but also eternal priests, a dignity far higher than kingship, because by that priesthood we are worthy to appear before God, to pray for others, and to teach one another mutually the things that are of God. For these are the duties of priests, and they cannot possibly be permitted to any unbeliever. Christ has gained for us this favor, if we believe in him, that just as we are his brethren and coheirs and fellow kings with him, so we should be also fellow priests with him and venture with confidence through the spirit of faith to come into the presence of God and cry "Abba, Father!" and to pray for one another, and to do all things that we see done and figured in the visible and earthly office of priesthood. But to an unbelieving person nothing renders service or works for good. He himself is in servitude to all things, and all things turn out for evil to him, because he uses all things in an impious way for his own advantage and not for the glory of God. And thus he is not a priest but a profane person whose prayers are turned into sin. Nor does he ever appear in the presence of God, because God does not hear sinners.

Who then can comprehend the loftiness of that Christian dignity that, by its royal power, rules over all things, even over death, life, and sin, and by its priestly glory is all powerful with

God, since God does what he himself seeks and wishes, as it is written: "He fulfills the desire of those who fear him; he also hears their cry and saves them" (Ps. 145:19). This glory certainly cannot be attained by any works but by faith only.

From these considerations anyone may clearly see how a Christian man is free from all things, so that he needs no works in order to be justified and saved but receives these gifts in abundance from faith alone. Indeed, were he so foolish as to pretend to be justified, set free, saved, and made a Christian by means of any good work, he would immediately lose faith with all its benefits. Such folly is well represented in the fable where a dog, running along in the water and carrying in his mouth a real piece of meat, is deceived by the reflection of the meat in the water and, in trying with open mouth to seize it, loses the meat and its image at the same time.

Here you will ask, "If all who are in the church are priests, by what character are those whom we now call priests to be distinguished from the laity?" I reply: By the use of these words, "priest," "clergy," "spiritual person," "ecclesiastics," an injustice has been done, since they have been transferred from the remaining body of Christians to those few who are now, by a hurtful custom, called ecclesiastics. For Holy Scripture makes no distinction between them, except that those who are now boastfully called popes, bishops, and lords it calls ministers, servants, and stewards who are to serve the rest in the ministry of the Word, for teaching the faith of Christ and the freedom of believers. For though it is true that we are all equally priests, we cannot—nor if we could, ought we all—minister and teach publicly. Thus Paul says, "This is how one should regard us, as servants of Christ and stewards of the mysteries of God" (1 Cor. 4:1).

This bad system has now issued in such a pompous display of power and such a terrible tyranny that no earthly government can be compared to it, as if the laity were something else than Christians. A perversion of things has taken place so that the knowledge of Christian grace, of faith, of liberty, and altogether of Christ has been utterly destroyed and has been followed by an intolerable slavery to human works and laws. And, according to the Lamentations of Jeremiah, we have become the slaves of the worst men on earth, who abuse our misery to all the disgraceful and ignominious purposes of their own will.

Returning to the subject that we had begun, I think it has been made clear by these considerations that it is not sufficient, nor a Christian course, to preach the works, life, and words of Christ in a purely historical manner—that is, as facts that it suffices to know as an example of how to frame our life, as do those who are now held to be the best preachers. For less is it sufficient to keep silence altogether on these things [Christ] and to instead teach the laws of men and the decrees of the fathers.[5] ...

Now preaching ought to have the object of promoting faith in him, so that he may not only be Christ but a Christ for you and for me, and that what is said of him and what he is called may work in us. And this faith is produced and is maintained by preaching why Christ came, what he has brought us and given to us, and to what profit and advantage he is to be received. This is done when the Christian liberty that we have from Christ himself is rightly taught and we are shown how all Christians are kings and priests and how we are lords of all things and may be confident that whatever we do in the presence of God is pleasing and acceptable to him.

Whose heart does not rejoice in its inmost core at hearing these things? Whose heart, on receiving so great a consolation,

---

5. "Fathers" here refers to the Christian theologians of the early church.

would not become sweet with the love of Christ, a love to which it can never attain by any laws or works? Who can injure such a heart or make it afraid? If the consciousness of sin or the horror of death rush in on it, it is prepared to hope in the Lord and is fearless of such evils and undisturbed until it shall look down on its enemies. For it believes that the righteousness of Christ is its own and that its sin is no longer its own but that of Christ, for on account of its faith in Christ, all its sin must be swallowed up from before the face of the righteousness of Christ, as I have said above. It learns too, with the apostle, to scoff at death and sin and to say, "'O death, where is your victory? O death, where is your sting?' The sting of death is sin, and the power of sin is the law. But thanks be to God, who gives us the victory through our Lord Jesus Christ" (1 Cor. 15:55–57). For death is swallowed up in victory—not only the victory of Christ, but ours also, since by faith it becomes ours and in it we too conquer.

Let it suffice to say this concerning the inner man and his liberty and concerning that righteousness of faith, which needs neither laws nor good works. Indeed, they are even hurtful to it if any one pretends to be justified by them.

Now let us turn to the other side, to the outward man. Here we shall give an answer to all those who, taking offense at the word of faith and at what I have asserted, say, "If faith does everything and by itself suffices for justification, why then are good works commanded? Are we then to take our ease and do no works, content with faith?" I respond: Not so, impious one, not so. That would indeed really be the case if we were thoroughly and completely inner and spiritual persons. But that will not happen until the last day, when the dead shall be raised. As long as we live in the flesh, we are but beginning and making advances in that which shall be completed in a future life. On this account the apostle calls that which we have in this life the firstfruits of the Spirit (Rom. 8:23). In the future we shall have the tenths and the fullness of the Spirit. Here is the place to assert what was stated above, that the Christian is the servant of all and subject to all. For in that part in which he is free he does no works, but in that in which he is a servant he does all works. Let us see on what principle this is so.

Although, as I have said, inwardly, and according to the spirit, a man is amply enough justified by faith, having all that he requires to have, except that this very faith and abundance ought to increase from day to day, even till the future life. Still, he remains in this mortal life on earth, in which it is necessary that he should rule his own body and have interactions with men. Here then works begin, here he must not take his ease, here he must give heed to exercise his body by fasts, vigils, labor, and other moderate disciplines, so that it may be subdued to the spirit and obey and conform itself to the inner man and faith and not rebel against them nor hinder them, as is its nature to do if it is not kept under. For the inner man, being conformed to God and created after the image of God through faith, rejoices and delights itself in Christ, in whom such blessings have been conferred on it, and hence has only this task before it, to serve God with joy and for nothing in free love.

In doing this he [the Christian] offends that contrary will in his own flesh, which is striving to serve the world and to seek its own gratification. This the spirit of faith cannot and will not bear but applies itself with cheerfulness and zeal to keep it down and restrain it. As Paul says, "For I delight in the law of God, in my inner being, but I see in my members another law waging war against the law of my mind and making me captive to the law of sin that dwells in my members" (Rom. 7:22–23). And again: "But I discipline my body and keep it under control, lest after preaching to others I myself should be disqualified" (1 Cor.

9:27). And: "Those who belong to Christ Jesus have crucified the flesh with its passions and desires" (Gal. 5:24).

These works, however, must not be done with any notion that by them a man can be justified before God. For faith, which alone is righteousness before God, will not bear with this false notion, but solely with this purpose, that the body may be brought into subjection and be purified from its evil lusts, so that our eyes may be turned only to purging away those lusts. For when the soul has been cleansed by faith and made to love God, it would have all things to be cleansed in like manner, and especially in its own body, so that all things might unite with it in the love and praise of God. Thus it comes that from the requirements of his own body a man cannot take his rest but is compelled on its account to do many good works that he may bring it into subjection. Yet these works are not the means of his justification before God; he does them out of disinterested love to the service of God, looking to no other end than to do what is well-pleasing to him whom he desires to obey dutifully in all things.

On this principle every man may easily instruct himself in what measure and with what distinctions he ought to chasten his own body. He will fast, watch, and labor just as much as he sees to suffice for keeping down the wantonness and sinful desires of the body. But those who pretend to be justified by works are looking not to the mortification of their lusts but only to the works themselves, thinking that, if they can accomplish as many works and as great ones as possible, all is well with them and they are justified. Sometimes they even injure their brain and extinguish nature, or at least make it useless. This is a tremendous mistake and ignorance of Christian life and faith, when a man seeks without faith to be justified and saved by works.

To make what we have said more easy to understand, let us explain by analogies. The works of a Christian, who is justified and saved by his faith out of the pure and unbought mercy of God, ought to be regarded in the same light as would have been those of Adam and Eve in Paradise, and of all their posterity, if they had not sinned. Of them it is said, "The LORD God took the man and put him in the garden of Eden to work it and keep it" (Gen. 2:15). Now Adam had been created by God just and righteous, so that he could not have needed to be justified and made righteous by keeping the garden and working in it. Nevertheless, so that he [Adam] might not be unemployed, God gave him the business of keeping and cultivating Paradise. These would have indeed been works of perfect freedom, being done for no other goal than that God might be pleased and not in order to obtain justification, which he already had to the full and which would have been innate in us all.

So it is with the works of a believer. Through faith he is restored to Paradise and created anew. He has no need for works for his justification, but that he may not be idle but may keep his own body and work on it. His works are to be done freely, with the sole object of pleasing God.

2

COMMENTARY ON GALATIANS

Faith and Works of the Law

Luther's Galatians commentary of 1531 is based on a series of lecture notes taken by his students in that year. It was ultimately edited and published with Luther's approval in 1535. It is sometimes called the "large" Galatians commentary because the reformer had already written an earlier, shorter edition in 1519.

This commentary is extremely important because it was written at a critical point in the history of the Reformation. A year earlier in the southern German city of Augsburg, the Lutheran princes of Germany (then part of the Holy Roman Empire) had presented their faith and proposals for reform to Emperor Charles V. This was the same emperor who had only nine years earlier condemned Luther as an outlaw at the Diet of Worms (1521). Luther was still an outlaw under imperial law and therefore could not attend the meeting at Augsburg. Instead, Philipp Melanchthon, Luther's co-reformer at Wittenberg, wrote and presented a confession of faith known as the Augsburg Confession.

Ultimately, the Lutheran princes' confession of faith was not accepted by the emperor. In fact, it was subjected to severe criticism by the Roman Catholic theologians present at the meeting. The next year, Melanchthon wrote a document (called the Apology to the Augsburg Confession) in response to this list of criticisms (known as the Papal Confutation). In light of the fact that the Catholic theologians were particularly critical of Luther's teaching of justification by faith alone, the largest portion of Melanchthon's defense was focused on this doctrine. Likewise, Luther had these criticisms in mind when lecturing on Galatians during the same year. For this reason, the 1531 Galatians commentary is viewed by many scholars as a partial defense of the Augsburg Confession, along with Melanchthon's Apology.

The selection from the Galatians commentary below discusses the contrast between the active works of the law and the passive trust of faith. In the theology of the medieval church, and indeed in contemporary Roman Catholicism, the claim is made that faith does not ultimately reconcile sinners with God. Rather, faith is only one element in a process through which God makes sinners able to merit their own salvation. According to this teaching, God's grace is a kind of power given to sinners by which they gain the ability to become obedient to God and merit salvation. This merit, along with the forgiveness brought about by Christ's death, allows humans to make their way to heaven. Therefore, from the Roman Catholic perspective, faith is one necessary foundation for this process to work, since it tells sinners to whom and to what end their meritorious works (that is, works of love) are to be directed (namely, God and the goal of gaining eternal fellowship with him). Nevertheless, in Roman Catholicism, faith alone is ultimately insufficient for salvation. Works of love must be added to faith to make it truly saving.

As Luther shows in the selection from the commentary below, this is a highly inaccurate way of reading Paul and indeed the whole of the New Testament. Paul states clearly that the works of the law in no way help us gain salvation. This is the case for two reasons. First, because of the sin of Adam, human beings are born sinful and therefore cannot hope to curry any favor with God. Only by the obedience of Jesus and his substitutionary death on the cross can sinners be reconciled with God through faith. Faith receives Christ's perfect righteousness, by which believers are both acquitted of sin and judged positively righteous before God. People who rely on their works will always ultimately fail to keep God's commandments perfectly and therefore cannot be saved.

Second, people of faith are the only true doers of the law. Although unbelievers can certainly be good citizens and go through the motions of performing external deeds in accordance with the law, God does not account them as righteous. As Scripture frequently notes, God is interested primarily in the disposition of the heart. The heart can only be purified by faith created by the work of the Holy Spirit.

When one has faith, one will perform the law out of true trust and love of God. Believers love and trust God because he has saved them through the work of Jesus. When people do good works merely to make God happy and thereby curry his favor, they act for selfish and insincere reasons. That is to say, whether consciously or unconsciously, they are only interested in using the goodness they do to other people in order to save themselves. Hence, only by taking away the threat and demand of the law and replacing it with God's unconditional love in the gospel is it possible for a person to come to truly obey God and his law. True obedience springs only from a grateful heart, not from one intent on gaining favor.

3:10. For all who rely on works of the law are under a curse . . .

The curse of God is like a flood that swallows everything that is not of faith. To avoid the curse we must hold on to the promise of the blessing in Christ. The reader is reminded that all this has no bearing on civil laws, customs, or political matters. Civil laws and ordinances have their place and purpose. Let every government enact the best possible laws. But civil righteousness will never deliver a person from the condemnation of God's law.

I have good reason for calling your attention to this. People easily mistake civil righteousness for spiritual righteousness. In civil life we must, of course, pay attention to laws and deeds, but in the spiritual life we must not think to be justified by laws and works but always keep in mind the promise and blessing of Christ, our only Savior.

According to Paul everything that is not of faith is sin. When our opponents hear us repeat this statement of Paul, they make it appear as if we taught that governments should not be honored, as if we favored rebellion against the constituted authorities, as if we condemned all laws. Our opponents do us a great wrong, for we make a clear-cut distinction between civil and spiritual affairs.

Governmental laws and ordinances are blessings of God for this life only. As for everlasting life, temporal blessings are not good enough. Unbelievers enjoy more temporal blessings than the Christians. Civil or legal righteousness may be good enough for this life but not for the life hereafter. Otherwise the unbelievers would be nearer heaven than the Christians, for unbelievers often excel in civil righteousness.

3:10. For it is written, "Cursed be everyone who does not abide by all things written in the Book of the Law, and do them."

Paul goes on to prove from this quotation out of the book of Deuteronomy that all men who are under the law are under the sentence of sin, of the wrath of God, and of everlasting death. Paul produces his proof in a roundabout way. He turns to the negative statement, "Cursed be everyone who does not abide by all things written in the Book of the Law, and do them." "For all who rely on works of the law are under a curse." These two statements, one by Paul and the other by Moses, appear to conflict. Paul declares, "Whosoever shall do the works of the Law is accursed." Moses declares, "Whosoever shall not do the works of the Law is accursed." How can these two contradictory statements be reconciled? How can the one statement prove the other? No person can hope to understand Paul unless he understands the article of justification. These two statements are not at all inconsistent.

We must bear in mind that to do the works of the law does not mean only to live up to the superficial requirements of the law but also to obey the spirit of the law to perfection. But where will you find the person who can do that? Let him step forward and we will praise him. Our opponents have their answer ready-made. They quote Paul's own statement in Romans 2:13, "It is ... the doers of the law who will be justified." Very well. But let us first find out who the doers of the law are. They call a "doer" of the law one who performs the law in its literal sense. This is not to "do" the law. This is to sin. When our opponents go about to perform the law, they sin against the first, the second, and the third commandments; in fact, they sin against the whole law. For God requires above all that we worship him in spirit and in faith. In observing the law for the purpose of obtaining righteousness without faith in Christ, these law-workers go against the law and against God. They deny the righteousness of God, his mercy, and his promises. They deny Christ and all his benefits.

In their ignorance of the true purpose of the law, the exponents of the law abuse the law, as Paul says in Romans 10:3: "For, being ignorant of the righteousness of God, and seeking to establish their own, they did not submit to God's righteousness." In their folly our opponents rush into the Scriptures, pick out a sentence here and a sentence there about the law, and imagine they know all about it. Their works-righteousness is plain idolatry and blasphemy against God. No wonder they abide under the curse of God.

Because God saw that we could not fulfill the law, he provided a way of salvation long before the law was ever given, a salvation that he promised to Abraham, saying, "In you shall all nations be blessed" [Gen. 12:3].

The very first thing for us to do is to believe in Christ. First, we must receive the Holy Spirit, who enlightens and sanctifies us so that we can begin to do the law—i.e., to love God and our neighbor. Now the Holy Spirit is not obtained by the law, but by faith in Christ. In the last analysis, to do the law means to believe in Jesus Christ. The tree comes first, and then come the fruits.

The Sophists[1] admit that a mere external and superficial performance of the law without sincerity and good will is plain hypocrisy. Judas acted like the other disciples. What was wrong with Judas? Note what Rome answers: "Judas was a reprobate. His motives were perverse, therefore his works were hypocritical and no good." Well, well. Rome does admit, after all, that works in themselves do not justify unless they issue from a sincere heart. Why do our opponents not profess the same truth in spiritual matters? There, above all, faith must precede everything. The heart must be purified by faith before a person can lift a finger to please God.

There are two classes of doers of the law, true doers and hypocritical doers. The true doers of the law are those who are moved by faith in Christ to do the law. The hypocritical doers of the law are those who seek to obtain righteousness by a mechanical performance of good works while their hearts are far removed from God. They act like the foolish carpenter who starts with the roof when he builds a house. Instead of

---

1. By "Sophists," Luther means the medieval theologians and contemporary Roman Catholic theologians. Originally, Sophists were professional rhetoric teachers in ancient Athens. Later, they became famous as the chief opponents of the Greek philosopher Socrates and later his student Plato. They were known for twisting words as a way of winning arguments. By applying this name to his Catholic opponents, Luther is implying that this is the practice of his adversaries as well.

doing the law, these law-conscious hypocrites break the law. They break the very first commandment of God by denying his promise in Christ. They do not worship God in faith. They worship themselves.

... The real doers of the law are the true believers. The Holy Spirit enables them to love God and their neighbor. But because we have only the firstfruits of the Spirit and not the tenth-fruits,[2] we do not observe the law perfectly. This imperfection of ours, however, is not imputed to us, for Christ's sake.

Hence, the statement of Moses, "Cursed be everyone who does not abide by all things written in the Book of the Law, and do them," is not contrary to Paul. Moses requires perfect doers of the law. But where will you find them? Nowhere. Moses himself confessed that he was not a perfect doer of the law. He said to the Lord, "Pardon our iniquity and our sin" [Exod. 34:9]. Christ alone can make us innocent of any transgression. How so? First, by the forgiveness of our sins and the imputation of his righteousness. Secondly, by the gift of the Holy Spirit, who engenders new life and activity in us.

Objections to the Doctrine of Faith Disproved

Here we shall take the time to enter upon the objections that our opponents raise against the doctrine of faith. There are many passages in the Bible that deal with works and the reward of works which our opponents cite against us in the belief that these will disprove the doctrine of faith that we teach.

The Sophists grant that according to the reasonable order of nature, being precedes doing. They grant that any act is faulty

2. By "tenth-fruits" Luther means the full gift of the Spirit, which will at the end of time allow resurrected believers to obey God perfectly. Such a total sanctification is not possible in this life.

unless it proceeds from a right motive. They grant that a person
must be right before he can do right. Why do they not grant
that the right inclination of the heart toward God through faith
in Christ must precede works?

In the eleventh chapter of the Epistle to the Hebrews we
find a catalogue of various works and deeds of the saints of the
Bible. David, who killed a lion and a bear and defeated Goliath,
is mentioned. In the heroic deeds of David the Sophist can
discover nothing more than outward achievement. But the
deeds of David must be evaluated according to the personality of David. When we understand that David was a man of
faith, whose heart trusted in the Lord, we shall understand
why he could do such heroic deeds. David said, "The LORD
who delivered me from the paw of the lion and from the paw
of the bear will deliver me from the hand of this Philistine."
Again: "You come to me with a sword and with a spear and
with a javelin, but I come to you in the name of the LORD
of hosts, the God of the armies of Israel, whom you have de-
fied. This day the LORD will deliver you into my hand, and
I will strike you down and cut off your head" (1 Sam. 17:37,
45–46). Before David could achieve a single heroic deed he
was already a man beloved of God, strong and constant in
faith.

Of Abel it is said in the same epistle, "By faith Abel offered
God a more excellent sacrifice than Cain" [Heb. 11:4]. When
the Sophists come upon the parallel passage in Genesis 4:4,
they get no further than the words, "And the LORD had regard for Abel and his offering." "Aha!" they cry. "See, God
has respect to offerings. Works do justify." With mud in their
eyes they cannot see that the text says in Genesis that the Lord
had respect to the person of Abel first. Abel pleased the Lord
because of his faith. Because the person of Abel pleased the

Lord, the offering of Abel pleased the Lord also. The Epistle to the Hebrews expressly states, "By faith Abel offered God a more excellent sacrifice."

In our dealings with God the work is worth nothing without faith, for "without faith it is impossible to please him" (Heb. 11:6). The sacrifice of Abel was better than the sacrifice of Cain because Abel had faith. As to Cain, he had no faith or trust in God's grace but strutted about in his own fancied worth. When God refused to recognize Cain's worth, Cain became angry at God and at Abel.

The Holy Spirit speaks of faith in different ways in the Sacred Scriptures. Sometimes he speaks of faith independently of other matters. When the Scriptures speak of faith in the absolute or abstract, faith refers to justification directly. But when the Scripture speaks of rewards and works, it speaks of compound or relative faith. We will furnish some examples: Galatians 5:6, "faith working through love"; Leviticus 18:5, "If a person does them, he shall live by them"; Matthew 19:17, "If you would enter life, keep the commandments"; Psalm 37:27, "Turn away from evil and do good; so shall you dwell forever." In these and other passages where mention is made of doing, the Scriptures always speak of a faithful doing, a doing inspired by faith. "Do this and you shall live" means [this]: first have faith in Christ, and Christ will enable you to do and to live.

In the Word of God all things that are attributed to works are attributable to faith. Faith is the divinity of works. Faith permeates all the deeds of the believer, as Christ's divinity permeated his humanity. Abraham was accounted righteous because faith pervaded his whole personality and his every action.

When you read how the fathers, prophets, and kings accomplished great deeds, remember to explain them as the Epistle to the Hebrews accounts for them: "who through faith conquered kingdoms, enforced justice, obtained promises, stopped the mouths of lions" (Heb. 11:33). In this way will we correctly interpret all those passages that seem to support the righteousness of works. The law is truly observed only through faith. Hence, every "holy," "moral" law-worker is accursed.

Supposing that this explanation will not satisfy the Sophists, supposing that they should completely wrap me up in their arguments (they cannot do it), I would rather be wrong and give all credit to Christ alone. Here is Christ. Paul, Christ's apostle, declares that "Christ redeemed us from the curse of the law by becoming a curse for us" (Gal. 3:13). I hear with my own ears that I cannot be saved except by the blood and death of Christ. I conclude, therefore, that it is up to Christ to overcome my sins and not up to the law or my own efforts. If he is the price of my redemption, if he was made sin for my justification, I do not care if a thousand Scripture passages for the righteousness of works are quoted against the righteousness of faith. I have the author and Lord of the Scriptures on my side. I would rather believe him than all that riffraff of "pious" law-workers.

3:11. Now it is evident that no one is justified before God by the law, for "The righteous shall live by faith."

The apostle draws into his argument the testimony of the prophet Habakkuk: "The righteous shall live by his faith" [2:4]. This passage carries much weight because it eliminates the law and the deeds of the law as factors in the process of our justification.

The Sophists misconstrue this passage by saying, "The righteous shall live by faith, if it is a working faith, or a faith formed and performed by works of love." Their annotation is a forgery. To speak of formed or unformed faith, a sort of double faith, is contrary to the Scriptures.[3] If works of love can form and perfect faith, I am forced to say eventually that deeds of love constitute the essential factor in the Christian religion.[4] Christ and his benefits would be lost to us.

3:12. But the law is not of faith.

In direct opposition to the Sophists Paul declares, "The law is not of faith." What is this "love" the Sophists talk so much about? Does not the law command love? The fact is the law commands nothing but charity, as we may gather from the following Scripture passages: "You shall love the LORD your God with all your heart and with all your soul and with all your might" (Deut. 6:5); ". . . showing steadfast love to thousands of those who love me and keep my commandments" (Exod. 20:6); "On these two commandments depend all the Law and the Prophets" (Matt. 22:40). If the law requires love, love is part of the law and not of faith. Since Christ has displaced the law, which commands love, it follows that love has been abrogated with the law as a factor in our justification, and only faith is left.

3:12. "The one who does them shall live by them."

Paul undertakes to explain the difference between the righteousness of the law and the righteousness of faith. The righteousness of the law is the fulfillment of the law according to the passage, "The one who does them shall live by them." The righteousness of faith is to believe the gospel according to the

---

3. What is being referred to here is the Roman Catholic theory that when Paul speaks of faith, he means faith along with the loving deeds, or good works that it produces. In other words, faith alone does not justify a sinner.

4. Here Luther does not mean that it is not important for Christians to obey the law and do loving deeds to the neighbor. Rather, he is rejecting the idea that works form any aspect of our relationship with God.

passage, "The righteous shall live by faith." The law is a statement of debit; the gospel a statement of credit. By this distinction Paul explains why charity, which is the commandment of the law, cannot justify, because the law contributes nothing to our justification.

Indeed, works do follow after faith, but faith is not therefore a meritorious work. Faith is a gift. The character and limitations of the law must be rigidly maintained.

When we believe in Christ, we live by faith. When we believe in the law, we may be active enough, but we have no life. The function of the law is not to give life. The function of the law is to kill. True, the law says, "The one who does them shall live by them." But where is the person who can do "them"—i.e., love God with all his heart, soul, and mind and his neighbor as himself?

Paul has nothing against those who are justified by faith and therefore are true doers of the law. He opposes those who think they can fulfill the law when in reality they can only sin against the law by trying to obtain righteousness by the law. The law demands that we fear, love, and worship God with a true faith. The law-workers fail to do this. Instead, they invent new modes of worship and new kinds of works that God never commanded. They provoke his anger according to the passage, "In vain do they worship me, teaching as doctrines the commandments of men" (Matt. 15:9). Hence, the law-righteous workers are downright rebels against God and idolaters who constantly sin against the first commandment. In short, they are no good at all though outwardly they seem to be extremely solicitous of the honor of God.

We who are justified by faith, as the saints of old, may be under the law, but we are not under the curse of the law because sin is not imputed to us for Christ's sake. If the law cannot be fulfilled by the believers, if sin continues to cling to them despite their love for God, what can you expect of people who are not yet justified by faith, who are still enemies of God and his Word, like the unbelieving law-workers? It goes to show how impossible it is for those who have not been justified by faith to fulfill the law.

SOLA GRATIA

3

PREFACE TO ST. PAUL'S LETTER TO THE ROMANS

In the year 1522, Luther returned to Wittenberg after spending a year in hiding at the Wartburg Castle. During his period of hiding, he had translated the New Testament into German. This was a significant event because although there had been previous translations of Scripture into the language of the common people, they were typically based on the corrupted Latin edition (called the Vulgate) used by the medieval church. To make his translation, Luther used the Humanist scholar Erasmus's 1516 edition of the Greek New Testament, which was based on the best manuscripts of the Greek New Testament available to private scholars at the time.

Luther took his task of biblical translation very seriously. Although he completed and published his translation of the New Testament in 1522, he continued revising and improving it for the rest of his life. By 1534, Luther had also successfully translated the Old Testament and published a full edition of the Bible. Although there were other earlier full German translations published in this period (for example, in Zurich in 1529), the Luther Bible eventually became the standard translation within the German-speaking world, in the same way that the King James Version eventually became the standard translation in the English-speaking world. Moreover, Luther's German translation was highly influential on the development and standardization of the German language itself. The so-called High German of Luther's Saxony spread and became the standard version of the language, largely because of Luther's use of it in his translation.

Along with Luther's translations, he also wrote a series of introductions to individual books of the Bible. Much like his Bible translation, these introductions had a significant cultural impact. Within the English Reformation, they formed the basis of the introductions written by William Tyndale for the first edition of his English translation of the Bible (the partial basis of the later KJV). Two centuries later, Luther's introduction to Paul's letter to the Romans (a full translation of which is printed below) also played a significant role in the spiritual awakening of the evangelist John Wesley, who famously "felt his heart strangely warmed" while listening to a public reading of it.

In this introduction to Romans, Luther gives a summary of the main topics of Paul's letter. Most importantly, Luther gives a full and systematic exposition of Paul's distinction between law and gospel. As Luther shows, God has revealed his law to the human race for a number of purposes. He has revealed the law in order to promote order in human society. Likewise, he has revealed his law in order to teach believers what works of love they should do in order to praise God and assist their neighbors. Nevertheless, neither of these functions of the law can justify and save human beings.

For those who seek to be justified by the law, the problem remains that God looks primarily at the human heart and only secondarily at external human works. Unfortunately, not only is it impossible for human beings to consistently obey the law with their external works, but the human heart is also permanently damaged by sin. Although fallen human beings can in a purely external sense discipline themselves and hold back their sinful impulses so as to appear righteous before other people, God looks at the heart. Therefore, he cannot view humans in their fallen state as anything other than utterly sinful. Ultimately, the root of all sin in the human heart is a lack of trust of God and his goodness. Because God sees this inner corruption, even when humans behave well in their external works, such outward righteousness is tainted by the inward lack of perfect trust and love of God.

Therefore, beyond promoting order and outward obedience, there is also another and, indeed, main function of the law. This is the use of the law as a mirror that reveals human corruption and God's wrath against it. The revelation of this divine wrath is ultimately not meant to condemn sinners to damnation but rather to show them their sickness so that God may serve as their physician. Hence, such a revelation of the law works repentance in sinful human beings and is therefore an essential aspect of the public preaching of the church.

The repentance brought about by the preaching of the law prepares sinners for the gospel. The gospel is not a new or higher law. Rather, it is God's promise that Christ has died and risen to redeem humanity. It is an unconditional promise that this salvation is a completed fact "for you." After the minister of the Word has proclaimed the law and worked repentance, the minister is to proclaim the unconditional promise of the gospel. Because the gospel is the living Word of God, God the Holy Spirit works through the hearing of the gospel to create faith in the hearts and minds of believers. As a result, they receive Christ's righteousness and are judged righteous before the law.

Moreover, since the Spirit has overcome unbelief (the ultimate root of sin) in those in whom he has created faith, he also sanctifies believers and energizes them for holy living. Holy living is never perfect in believers in this life. Out of weakness and temptation, believers continue to sin daily. Therefore, throughout their lives, believers must continuously repeat and trust in the righteousness of Christ imputed to them, until they are finally perfected in the kingdom of God.

This letter is truly the most important piece in the New Testament. It is purest gospel. It is worthwhile for a Christian not only to memorize it word for word but also to occupy himself with it daily, as though it were the daily bread of the soul. It is impossible to read or to meditate on this letter too much or too well. The more one deals with it, the more precious it becomes and the better it tastes. Therefore I want to carry out my service and, with this preface, provide an introduction to the letter, insofar as God gives me the ability, so that everyone can gain the fullest possible understanding of it. Up to now it has been darkened by glosses[1] and by many a useless comment, but it is in itself a bright light, almost bright enough to illumine the entire Scripture.

To begin with, we have to become familiar with the vocabulary of the letter and know what St. Paul means by the words law, sin, grace, faith, justice, flesh, spirit, etc. Otherwise there is no use in reading it.

You must not understand the word "law" here in human fashion—i.e., a regulation about what sort of works must be done or must not be done. That is the way it is with human laws: you satisfy the demands of the law with works, whether your heart is in it or not. God judges what is in the depths of the heart. Therefore his law also makes demands on the depths of the heart and does not let the heart rest content in works. Rather, it punishes as hypocrisy and lies all works done apart from the depths of the heart. All human beings are called liars (Ps. 116[:11]), since none of them keeps or can keep God's law from the depths of the heart. Everyone finds inside himself an aversion to good and a craving for evil. Where there is no free desire for good, there the heart has not set itself on God's law. There also sin is surely to be found, and the deserved wrath of God, whether many good works and an honorable life appear outwardly or not.

Therefore in chapter 2, St. Paul adds that the Jews are all sinners and says that only the doers of the law are justified in the

---

1. A "gloss" is a notation in the margins of medieval Bibles. They gave explanations of the meaning of texts. Here Luther is suggesting that various glosses have covered over the simple meaning of the text of the Bible.

sight of God. What he is saying is that no one is a doer of the law by works. On the contrary, he says to them, "You teach that one should not commit adultery, and you commit adultery. You judge another in a certain matter and condemn yourselves in that same matter, because you do the very same thing that you judged in another." It is as if he were saying, "Outwardly you live quite properly in the works of the law and judge those who do not live the same way; you know how to teach everybody. You see the speck in another's eye but do not notice the beam in your own."

Outwardly you keep the law with works out of fear of punishment or love of gain. Likewise you do everything without free desire and love of the law; you act out of aversion and force. You would rather act otherwise if the law did not exist. It follows, then, that you, in the depths of your heart, are an enemy of the law. What do you mean, therefore, by teaching another not to steal when you, in the depths of your heart, are a thief and would be one outwardly too, if you dared (of course, outward work does not last long with such hypocrites)? So then, you teach others but not yourself. You do not even know what you are teaching; indeed, you have never understood the law rightly. Furthermore, the law increases sin, as St. Paul says in chapter 5. That is because a person becomes more and more an enemy of the law the more it demands of him what he cannot possibly do.

In chapter 7, St. Paul says, "The law is spiritual" [v. 14]. What does that mean? If the law were physical, then it could be satisfied by works, but since it is spiritual, no one can satisfy it unless everything he does springs from the depths of the heart. But no one can give such a heart except the Spirit of God, who makes the person be like the law, so that he actually conceives a heartfelt longing for the law and henceforward does everything not through fear or coercion but from a free heart. Such a law is spiritual since it can only be loved and fulfilled by such a heart and such a spirit. If the Spirit is not in the heart, then there remain sin, aversion, and enmity against the law, which in itself is good, just, and holy.

You must get used to the idea that it is one thing to do the works of the law and quite another to fulfill it. The works of the law are everything that a person does or can do of his own free will and by his own powers to obey the law. But because in doing such works the heart abhors the law and yet is forced to obey it, the works are a total loss and are completely useless. That is what St. Paul means in chapter 3 when he says, "No human being is justified before God through the works of the law." From this you can see that the Schoolmasters and Sophists[2] are seducers when they teach that you can prepare yourself for grace by means of works. How can anybody prepare himself for good by means of works if he does no good work except with aversion and constraint in his heart? How can such a work please God if it proceeds from an averse and unwilling heart?

But to fulfill the law means to do its work eagerly, lovingly, and freely, without the constraint of the law; it means to live well and in a manner pleasing to God, as though there were no law or punishment. It is the Holy Spirit, however, who puts such eagerness of unconstrained love into the heart, as Paul says in chapter 5. But the Spirit is given only in, with, and through faith in Jesus Christ, as Paul says in his introduction. So, too, faith comes only through the Word of God, the gospel that preaches Christ—how he is both Son of God and man, how he died and rose for our sake. Paul says all this in chapters 3, 4, and 10.

2. The terms "Schoolmasters" and "Sophists" refer to medieval and contemporary Roman Catholic theologians.

That is why faith alone makes someone just and fulfills the law; it is faith that brings the Holy Spirit through the merits of Christ. The Spirit, in turn, renders the heart glad and free, as the law demands. Then good works proceed from faith itself. That is what Paul means in chapter 3 when, after he has thrown out the works of the law, he sounds as though he wants to abolish the law by faith. No, he says, we uphold the law through faith— i.e., we fulfill it through faith.

"Sin" in the Scriptures means not only external works of the body but also all those movements within us that stir themselves up and move us to do the external works—namely, the depth of the heart with all its powers. Therefore the word "do" should refer to a person's completely falling into sin. No external work of sin happens, after all, unless a person commits himself to it completely, body and soul. In particular, the Scriptures see into the heart, to the root and main source of all sin: unbelief in the depth of the heart. Thus, even as faith alone makes just and brings the Spirit and the desire to do good external works, so it is only unbelief that sins and exalts the flesh and brings desire to do evil external works. That is what happened to Adam and Eve in Paradise (cf. Gen. 3).

That is why only unbelief is called sin by Christ, as he says in John 16[:8–9]: "He [the Holy Spirit] will convict the world concerning sin . . . because they do not believe in me." Furthermore, before good or bad works happen, which are the good or bad fruits of the heart, there has to be present in the heart either faith or unbelief, the root, sap, and chief power of all sin. That is why, in the Scriptures, unbelief is called the head of the serpent and of the ancient dragon that the offspring of the woman (i.e., Christ) must crush, as was promised to Adam (cf. Gen. 3).

"Grace" and "gift" differ in that grace actually denotes God's kindness or favor that he has toward us and by which he is disposed to pour Christ and the Spirit with his gifts into us, as becomes clear from chapter 5, where Paul says that grace and gift are in Christ, etc. The gifts and the Spirit increase daily in us, yet they are not complete, since evil desires and sins remain in us, which war against the Spirit, as Paul says in chapter 7, and in Galatians chapter 5. And Genesis chapter 3 proclaims the enmity between the offspring of the woman and that of the serpent. But grace does do this much: that we are accounted completely just before God. God's grace is not divided into bits and pieces, as are the gifts, but grace takes us up completely into God's favor for the sake of Christ, our intercessor and mediator, so that the gifts may begin their work in us.

In this way, then, you should understand chapter 7, where St. Paul portrays himself as still a sinner, while in chapter 8 he says that, because of the incomplete gifts and because of the Spirit, there is nothing damnable in those who are in Christ. Because our flesh has not been killed, we are still sinners, but because we believe in Christ and have the beginnings of the Spirit, God so shows us his favor and mercy that he neither notices nor judges such sins. Rather, he deals with us according to our belief in Christ until sin is killed.

Faith is not that human illusion and dream that some people think it is. When they hear and talk a lot about faith and yet see that no moral improvement and no good works result from it, they fall into error and say, "Faith is not enough. You must do works if you want to be virtuous and get to heaven." The result is that, when they hear the gospel, they stumble and make for themselves with their own powers a concept in their hearts that says, "I believe." This concept they hold to be true faith. But since it is a human fabrication and thought and not an experience of the heart, it accomplishes nothing, and there follows no improvement.

Faith is a work of God in us, which changes us and brings us to birth anew from God (cf. John 1). It kills the old Adam, makes us completely different people in heart, mind, senses, and all our powers, and brings the Holy Spirit with it. What a living, creative, active, powerful thing is faith! It is impossible that faith should ever stop doing good works. Faith does not ask whether good works are to be done, but before it is asked, it has done them. It is always active. Whoever does not do such works is without faith; he gropes and searches about him for faith and good works but doesn't know what faith or good works are. Even so, he chatters on with a great many words about faith and good works.

Faith is a living, unshakeable confidence in God's grace; it is so certain that someone would die a thousand times for it. This kind of trust in and knowledge of God's grace makes a person joyful, confident, and happy with regard to God and all creatures. This is what the Holy Spirit does by faith. Through faith, a person will do good to everyone without coercion, willingly and happily; he will serve everyone, suffer everything, for the love and praise of God who has shown him such grace. It is as impossible to separate works from faith as burning and shining from fire. Therefore be on guard against your own false ideas and against the chatterers who think they are clever enough to make judgments about faith and good works but who are in reality the biggest fools. Ask God to work faith in you; otherwise you will remain eternally without faith, no matter what you try to do or fabricate.

Now "justice"[3] is just such a faith. It is called God's justice or that justice which is valid in God's sight, because it is God who gives it and reckons it as justice for the sake of Christ our

---

3. Or "righteousness."

Mediator. It influences a person to give to everyone what he
owes him. Through faith a person becomes sinless and eager
for God's commands. Thus he gives God the honor due him
and pays him what he owes him. He serves people willingly
with the means available to him. In this way he pays everyone
his due. Neither nature nor free will nor our own powers can
bring about such a justice, for even as no one can give himself
faith, so too he cannot remove unbelief. How can he then take
away even the smallest sin? Therefore everything that takes place
outside faith or in unbelief is lie, hypocrisy, and sin (Rom. 14),
no matter how smoothly it may seem to go.

   You must not understand flesh here as denoting only unchastity, or spirit as denoting only the inner heart. Here St.
Paul calls flesh (as does Christ in John 3) everything born of
flesh—i.e., the whole human being with body and soul, reason
and senses, since everything in him tends toward the flesh. That
is why you should know enough to call that person "fleshly"
who, without grace, fabricates, teaches, and chatters about high
spiritual matters. You can learn the same thing from Galatians
chapter 5, where St. Paul calls heresy and hatred works of the
flesh. And in Romans chapter 8 he says that through the flesh
the law is weakened. He says this not of unchastity but of all
sins, most of all of unbelief, which is the most spiritual of vices.

   On the other hand, you should know enough to call that
person "spiritual" who is occupied with the most outward of
works as was Christ, when he washed the feet of the disciples,
and Peter, when he steered his boat and fished. So then, a
person is "flesh" who, inwardly and outwardly, lives only to
do those things that are of use to the flesh and to temporal
existence. A person is "spirit" who, inwardly and outwardly,
lives only to do those things that are of use to the spirit and
to the life to come.

Unless you understand these words in this way, you will never understand either this letter of St. Paul or any book of the Scriptures. Be on guard, therefore, against any teacher who uses these words differently, no matter who he be, whether Jerome, Augustine, Ambrose, Origen, or anyone else as great as or greater than they.[4] Now let us turn to the letter itself.

The first duty of a preacher of the gospel is, through his revealing of the law and of sin, to rebuke and to turn into sin everything in life that does not have the Spirit and faith in Christ as its base. Thereby he will lead people to a recognition of their miserable condition, and thus they will become humble and yearn for help. This is what St. Paul does. He begins in chapter 1 by rebuking the gross sins and unbelief that are in plain view, as were (and still are) the sins of the pagans, who live without God's grace. He says that through the gospel God is revealing his wrath from heaven on all mankind because of the godless and unjust lives they live. For, although they know and recognize day by day that there is a God, human nature in itself, without grace, is so evil that it neither thanks nor honors God. This nature blinds itself and continually falls into wickedness, even going so far as to commit idolatry and other horrible sins and vices. It is unashamed of itself and leaves such things unpunished in others.

In chapter 2, St. Paul extends his rebuke to those who appear outwardly pious or who sin secretly. Such were the Jews, and such are all hypocrites still who live virtuous lives but without eagerness and love; in their hearts they are enemies of God's law and like to judge other people. That is the way with hypocrites: they think that they are pure but are actually full of greed, hate,

4. The names Jerome, Augustine, Ambrose, and Origen refer to famous and widely read theologians from the early church.

pride, and all sorts of filth (cf. Matt. 23). These are they who despise God's goodness and, by their hardness of heart, heap wrath on themselves. Thus Paul explains the law rightly when he lets no one remain without sin but proclaims the wrath of God to all who want to live virtuously by nature or by free will. He makes them out to be no better than public sinners; he says they are hard of heart and unrepentant.

In chapter 3, Paul lumps both secret and public sinners together: the one, he says, is like the other; all are sinners in the sight of God. Besides, the Jews had God's Word, even though many did not believe in it. But still God's truth and faith in him are not thereby rendered useless. St. Paul introduces, as an aside, the saying from Psalm 51 that God remains true to his words. Then he returns to his topic and proves from Scripture that they are all sinners and that no one becomes just through the works of the law but that God gave the law only so that sin might be perceived.

Next St. Paul teaches the right way to be virtuous and to be saved; he says that they are all sinners, unable to glory in God. They must, however, be justified through faith in Christ, who has merited this for us by his blood and has become for us a mercy seat [cf. Exod. 25:17; Lev. 16:14–16; and 1 John 2:2] in the presence of God, who forgives us all our previous sins. In so doing, God proves that it is his justice alone, which he gives through faith, that helps us, the justice that was at the appointed time revealed through the gospel and, previous to that, was witnessed to by the Law and the Prophets. Therefore the law is set up by faith, but the works of the law, along with the glory taken in them, are knocked down by faith.

In chapters 1 to 3, St. Paul has revealed sin for what it is and has taught the way of faith that leads to justice. Now in chapter 4 he deals with some objections and criticisms. He takes up first the one that people raise who, on hearing that faith makes just without works, say, "What? Should we not do any good works?" Here St. Paul holds up Abraham as an example. He says, "What did Abraham accomplish with his good works? Were they all good for nothing and useless?" He concludes that Abraham was made righteous apart from all his works by faith alone. Even before the "work" of his circumcision, Scripture praises him as being just on account of faith alone (cf. Gen. 15). Now if the work of his circumcision did nothing to make him just, a work that God had commanded him to do and hence a work of obedience, then surely no other good work can do anything to make a person just. Even as Abraham's circumcision was an outward sign with which he proved his justice based on faith, so too all good works are only outward signs that flow from faith and are the fruits of faith; they prove that the person is already inwardly just in the sight of God.

St. Paul verifies his teaching on faith in chapter 3 with a powerful example from Scripture. He calls as witness David, who says in Psalm 32[:1–2, 5] that a person becomes just without works but does not remain without works once he has become just. Then Paul extends this example and applies it against all other works of the law. He concludes that the Jews cannot be Abraham's heirs just because of their blood relationship to him and still less because of the works of the law. Rather, they have to inherit Abrahams's faith if they want to be his real heirs, since it was prior to the law of Moses and the law of circumcision that Abraham became just through faith and was called a father of all believers. St. Paul adds that the law brings about more wrath than grace, because no one obeys it with love and eagerness. More disgrace than grace comes from the works of the law. Therefore faith alone can obtain the grace promised to Abraham. Examples like these are written for our sake that we also should have faith.

In chapter 5, St. Paul comes to the fruits and works of faith—namely, joy, peace, love for God and for all people; in addition, assurance, steadfastness, confidence, courage, and hope in sorrow and suffering. All of these follow where faith is genuine, because of the overflowing good will that God has shown in Christ: he had him die for us before we could ask him for it, yes, even while we were still his enemies. Thus we have established that faith, without any good works, makes just. It does not follow from that, however, that we should not do good works; rather, it means that morally upright works do not remain lacking. About such works the "works-holy" people know nothing; they invent for themselves their own works in which are neither peace nor joy nor assurance nor love nor hope nor steadfastness nor any kind of genuine Christian works or faith.

Next St. Paul makes a digression, a pleasant little side trip, and relates where both sin and justice, death and life come from. He opposes these two: Adam and Christ. What he wants to say is that Christ, a second Adam, had to come in order to make us heirs of his justice through a new spiritual birth in faith, just as the old Adam made us heirs of sin through the old fleshy birth.

St. Paul proves, by this reasoning, that a person cannot help himself by his works to get from sin to justice any more than he can prevent his own physical birth. St. Paul also proves that the divine law, which should have been well suited, if anything was, for helping people to obtain justice, not only was no help at all when it did come, but it even increased sin. Evil human nature, consequently, becomes more hostile to it; the more the law forbids it to indulge its own desires, the more it wants to. Thus the law makes Christ all the more necessary and demands more grace to help human nature.

In chapter 6, St. Paul takes up the special work of faith, the struggle that the spirit wages against the flesh to kill off those sins and desires that remain after a person has been made just. He teaches us that faith does not so free us from sin that we can be idle, lazy, and self-assured, as though there were no more sin in us. Sin is there, but because of faith that struggles against it, God does not reckon sin as deserving damnation. Therefore we have in our own selves a lifetime of work cut out for us; we have to tame our body, kill its lusts, force its members to obey the spirit and not the lusts. We must do this so that we may conform to the death and resurrection of Christ and complete our baptism, which signifies a death to sin and a new life of grace. Our aim is to be completely clean from sin and then to rise bodily with Christ and live forever.

St. Paul says that we can accomplish all this because we are in grace and not in the law. He explains that to be "outside the law" is not the same as having no law and being able to do what you please. No, being "under the law" means living without grace, surrounded by the works of the law. Then surely sin reigns by means of the law, since no one is naturally well-disposed toward the law. That very condition, however, is the greatest sin. But grace makes the law lovable to us, so there is then no sin anymore, and the law is no longer against us but one with us.

This is true freedom from sin and from the law. St. Paul writes about this for the rest of the chapter. He says it is a freedom only to do good with eagerness and to live a good life without the coercion of the law. This freedom is, therefore, a spiritual freedom that does not suspend the law but that supplies what the law demands—namely, eagerness and love. These silence the law so that it has no further cause to drive people on and make demands of them. It is as though you owed something to a moneylender and could not pay him. You could be rid of him in one of two ways: either he would take nothing from you and would tear up his account book, or a pious man would pay for you and give you what you needed to satisfy your debt. That is exactly how Christ freed us from the law. Therefore our freedom is not a wild, fleshy freedom that has no obligation to do anything. On the contrary, it is a freedom that does a great deal, indeed everything, yet is free of the law's demands and debts.

In chapter 7, St. Paul confirms the foregoing by an analogy drawn from married life. When a man dies, the wife is free; the one is free and clear of the other. It is not the case that the woman may not or should not marry another man; rather, she is now for the first time free to marry someone else. She could not do this before she was free of her first husband. In the same way, our conscience is bound to the law so long as our condition is that of the sinful old man. But when the old man is killed by the Spirit, then the conscience is free, and conscience and law are quit of each other. Not that conscience should now do nothing; rather, it should now for the first time truly cling to its second husband, Christ, and bring forth the fruit of life.

Next St. Paul sketches further the nature of sin and the law. It is the law that makes sin really active and powerful, because the old man becomes more and more hostile to the law since he cannot pay the debt demanded by the law. Sin is his very nature; of himself he cannot do otherwise. And so the law is his death and torture. Now the law is not itself evil; it is our evil nature that cannot tolerate that the good law should demand good from it. It is like the case of a sick person who cannot tolerate that you demand that he run and jump around and do other things that a healthy person does.

St. Paul concludes here that if we understand the law properly and comprehend it in the best possible way, then we will see that its sole function is to remind us of our sins, to kill us by our sins, and to make us deserving of eternal wrath. Conscience learns and experiences all this in detail when it comes face-to-face with the law. It follows, then, that we must have something else, over and above the law, that can make a person virtuous and cause him to be saved. Those, however, who do not understand the law rightly are blind; they go their way boldly and think they are satisfying the law with works. They do not know how much the law demands—namely, a free, willing, eager heart. That is the reason that they do not see Moses rightly before their eyes. For them he is covered and concealed by the veil.

Then St. Paul shows how spirit and flesh struggle with each other in one person. He gives himself as an example, so that we may learn how to kill sin in ourselves. He gives both spirit and flesh the name "law," so that just as it is in the nature of divine law to drive a person on and make demands of him, so too the flesh drives and demands and rages against the spirit and wants to have its own way. Likewise the spirit drives and demands against the flesh and wants to have its own way. This feud lasts in us for as long as we live, in one person more, in another less, depending on whether spirit or flesh is stronger. Yet the whole human being is both: spirit and flesh. The human being fights with himself until he becomes completely spiritual.

In chapter 8, St. Paul comforts fighters such as these and tells them that this flesh will not bring them condemnation. He goes on to show what the nature of flesh and spirit are. Spirit, he says, comes from Christ, who has given us his Holy Spirit; the Holy Spirit makes us spiritual and restrains the flesh. The Holy Spirit assures us that we are God's children no matter how furiously sin may rage within us, so long as we follow the Spirit and struggle against sin in order to kill it. Because nothing is so effective in deadening the flesh as the cross and suffering, Paul comforts us in our suffering. He says that the Spirit, love, and all creatures will stand by us; the Spirit in us groans and all creatures long with us that we be freed from the flesh and from sin. Thus we see that these three chapters—6, 7, and 8—all deal with the one work of faith, which is to kill the old Adam and to constrain the flesh.

In chapters 9, 10, and 11, St. Paul teaches us about the eternal providence of God. It is the original source that determines who will believe and who will not, who can be set free from sin and who cannot. Such matters have been taken out of our hands and are put into God's hands so that we might become virtuous. It is absolutely necessary that it be so, for we are so weak and unsure of ourselves that, if it depended on us, no human being would be saved. The devil would overpower all of us. But God is steadfast; his providence will not fail, and no one can prevent its realization. Therefore we have hope against sin.

But here we must shut the mouths of those sacrilegious and arrogant spirits who, mere beginners that they are, bring their reason to bear on this matter and commence, from their exalted position, to probe the abyss of divine providence and uselessly trouble themselves about whether they are predestined or not. These people must surely plunge to their ruin, since they will either despair or abandon themselves to a life of chance.

You, however, follow the reasoning of this letter in the order in which it is presented. Fix your attention first of all on Christ and the gospel, so that you may recognize your sin and his grace. Then struggle against sin, as chapters 1–8 have taught you to. Finally, when you have come, in chapter 8, under the shadow of the cross and suffering, they will teach you, in chapters 9–11, about providence and what a comfort it is. Apart from suffering, the cross, and the pangs of death, you cannot come to grips with providence without harm to yourself and secret anger against God. The old Adam must be quite dead before you can endure this matter and drink this strong wine. Therefore make sure you do not drink wine while you are still a babe at the breast. There is a proper measure, time, and age for understanding every doctrine.

In chapter 12, St. Paul teaches the true liturgy and makes all Christians priests, so that they may offer not money or cattle as priests do in the law but their own bodies, by putting their desires to death. Next he describes the outward conduct of Christians whose lives are governed by the Spirit; he tells how they teach, preach, rule, serve, give, suffer, love, live, and act toward friend, foe, and everyone. These are the works that a Christian does, for as I have said, faith is not idle.

In chapter 13, St. Paul teaches that one should honor and obey the secular authorities. He includes this not because it makes people virtuous in the sight of God but because it does ensure that the virtuous have outward peace and protection and that the wicked cannot do evil without fear and in undisturbed peace. Therefore it is the duty of virtuous people to honor secular authority, even though they do not, strictly speaking, need it. Finally, St. Paul sums up everything in love and gathers it all into the example of Christ: what he has done for us, we must also do and follow after him.

In chapter 14, St. Paul teaches that one should carefully guide those with weak conscience and spare them. One should not use Christian freedom to harm but rather to help the weak. Where that is not done, there follow dissention and despising of the gospel, on which everything else depends. It is better to give way a little to the weak in faith until they become stronger than to have the teaching of the gospel perish completely. This work is a particularly necessary work of love especially now when people, by eating meat and by other freedoms, are brashly, boldly, and unnecessarily shaking weak consciences that have not yet come to know the truth.

In chapter 15, St. Paul cites Christ as an example to show that we must also have patience with the weak, even those who fail by sinning publicly or by their disgusting morals. We must not cast them aside but must bear with them until they become better. That is the way Christ treated us and still treats us every day; he puts up with our vices, our wicked morals, and all our imperfection, and he helps us ceaselessly. Finally, Paul prays for the Christians at Rome; he praises them and commends them to God. He points out his own office and the message that he preaches. He makes an unobtrusive plea for a contribution for the poor in Jerusalem. Unalloyed love is the basis of all he says and does.

The last chapter consists of greetings. But Paul also includes a salutary warning against human doctrines that are preached alongside the gospel and that do a great deal of harm. It is as though he had clearly seen that out of Rome and through the Romans would come the deceitful, harmful Canons and Decretals[5] along with the entire brood and swarm of human laws and commands that is now drowning the whole world and has blotted out this letter and the whole of the Scriptures along with the Spirit and faith. Nothing remains but the idol Belly, and St. Paul depicts those people here as its servants. God deliver us from them. Amen.

We find in this letter, then, the richest possible teaching about what a Christian should know: the meaning of law, gospel, sin, punishment, grace, faith, justice, Christ, God, good works, love, hope, and the cross. We learn how we are to act toward everyone, toward the virtuous and sinful, toward the strong

---

5. Luther here is referring to the laws promulgated by the Roman Catholic Church in the Middle Ages. These laws are viewed as harmful by Luther, in that they were contrary to God's law in Scripture and sought to take over civil governance from secular authorities that God had established.

and the weak, [toward] friend and foe, and toward ourselves. Paul bases everything firmly on Scripture and proves his points with examples from his own experience and from the Prophets, so that nothing more could be desired. Therefore it seems that St. Paul, in writing this letter, wanted to compose a summary of the whole of Christian and evangelical teaching that would also be an introduction to the whole Old Testament. Without doubt, whoever takes this letter to heart possesses the light and power of the Old Testament. Therefore each and every Christian should make this letter the habitual and constant object of his study. God grant us his grace to do so. Amen.

4

THE THIRD ARTICLE
OF THE APOSTLES' CREED

The Work of the Holy Spirit

In the late 1520s, Luther's colleagues at Wittenberg and other government officials undertook a series of visitations to country parishes to inspect the state of Christian belief and practice among the clergy and the common people. What they discovered horrified them. Most of the common people, and indeed, many members of the clergy, did not know or understand the basic teachings of Christianity, much less the reforms proposed by the Reformation.

In order to help remedy this situation, the reformers at Wittenberg undertook a number of measures. Chief among these was the production of the Large and Small Catechisms by Luther. The Small Catechism contained a series of pithy summaries of basic Christian beliefs and practices. Such explanations were in no way intended to supplant the Bible as the supreme authority of Christian teaching. Rather, such a work was merely intended to give a brief summary of Scripture's content and prepare readers to participate in Christian worship and a deeper study of the Bible.

The Small Catechism contained explanations of the Ten Commandments, the Apostles' Creed, the Lord's Prayer, and the sacraments. The Large Catechism gave longer explanations of the same subjects and was intended to function as something of a sixteenth-century "leader's guide." The father of a household or estate was to read the Large Catechism in order to prepare himself to teach the content of the Small Catechism to both his other family members and, in some cases, the family servants.

The selection below is from the section of the Large Catechism that discusses the third article of the Apostles' Creed. The Apostles' Creed is an early Christian creed that was spoken as a confession of faith at the time of baptism. It summarizes the teaching of Scripture concerning the Triune God's works in creation, redemption, and sanctification. The third article deals with the Holy Spirit's work in the church and in the coming of God's eternal kingdom at the end of time.

As Luther shows, the Holy Spirit works to create faith through the preaching of the Word. In so doing, he gathers, forgives, and sanctifies believers within the Christian church. Unlike Roman Catholics, Luther did not believe that the church was primarily an institution but rather the gathering together of all those who have faith in Christ. This same Holy Spirit who brings believers to the true faith in the present age will also at the end of time raise and glorify the dead in their physical bodies. He does this all by the grace of his own unconditional love.

I believe in the Holy Spirit; the holy Christian church, the communion of saints; the forgiveness of sins; the resurrection of the body; and the life everlasting. Amen.

This article (as I have said) I cannot relate better than to sanctification. In this article the Holy Spirit, with his office, is declared and depicted—namely, that he makes holy. Therefore we must take our stand on the word "Holy Spirit" because it is so precise and comprehensive that we cannot find another. For there are, besides, many kinds of spirits mentioned in the Holy Scriptures, such as the spirit of man, heavenly spirits, and evil spirits. But the Spirit of God alone is called Holy Spirit—that is, he who has sanctified and still sanctifies us. For as the Father is called Creator, the Son, Redeemer, so the Holy Spirit, from his work, must be called Sanctifier, or One that makes holy. But how is such sanctifying done? Answer: Just as the Son obtains dominion, whereby he wins us, through his birth, death, resurrection, etc., so also the Holy Spirit effects our sanctification by the following parts: namely, by the communion of saints or the Christian church, the forgiveness of sins, the resurrection of the body, and the life everlasting; that is, he first leads us into his holy congregation, and places us in the bosom of the church, whereby he preaches to us and brings us to Christ.

For neither you nor I could ever know anything of Christ, or believe on him, and obtain him for our Lord unless it were offered to us and granted to our hearts by the Holy Spirit through the preaching of the gospel. The work is done and accomplished, for Christ has acquired and gained the treasure for us by his suffering, death, resurrection, etc. But if the work remained concealed so that no one knew of it, then it would be in vain and lost. That this treasure, therefore, might not lie buried but be appropriated and enjoyed, God has caused the Word to go forth and be proclaimed, in which he gives the Holy Spirit to bring this treasure home and appropriate it to us. Therefore sanctifying is nothing else than bringing us to Christ to receive this good, to which we could not attain of ourselves.

Learn, then, to understand this article most clearly. If you are asked, What do you mean by the words "I believe in the Holy Spirit"? you can answer, I believe that the Holy Spirit makes me holy, as his name implies. But whereby does he accomplish this, or what are his method and means to this end? Answer: By the Christian church, the forgiveness of sins, the resurrection of the body, and the life everlasting. For, in the first place, he has a peculiar congregation in the world, which is the mother that begets and bears every Christian through the Word of God, which he reveals and preaches [and through which] he illumines and enkindles hearts that they understand, accept it, cling to it, and persevere in it.

For where he does not cause it to be preached and made alive in the heart so that it is understood, it is lost, as was the case under the papacy, where faith was entirely put under the bench and no one recognized Christ as his Lord or the Holy Spirit as his Sanctifier; that is, no one believed that Christ is our Lord in the sense that he has acquired this treasure for us, without our works and merit, and made us acceptable to the Father. What, then, was lacking? This, that the Holy Spirit was not there to reveal it and cause it to be preached; but men and evil spirits were there, who taught us to obtain grace and be saved by our works. Therefore it is not a Christian church either; for where Christ is not preached, there is no Holy Spirit who creates, calls, and gathers the Christian church, without which no one can come to Christ the Lord. Let this suffice concerning the sum of this article. But because the parts that are here enumerated are not quite clear to the simple, we shall run over them also.

The Creed denominates the holy Christian church *communionem sanctorum*, a communion of saints; for both expressions, taken together, are identical. But formerly the one [the second] expression was not there, and it has been poorly and unintelligibly translated into German "a communion of saints" [*eine Gemeinschaft der Heiligen*]. If it is to be rendered plainly, it must be expressed quite differently in the German idiom; for the word *ecclesia* properly means in German "an assembly" [*eine Versammlung*]. But we are accustomed to the word "church," by which the simple do not understand an assembled multitude, but the consecrated house or building, although the house ought not to be called a church, except only for the reason that the multitude assembles there. For we who assemble there make and choose for ourselves a particular place and give a name to the house according to the assembly.

Thus the word "church" [*Kirche*] means really nothing else than a common assembly and is not German by idiom but Greek (as is also the word *ecclesia*); for in their own language they call it *kyria*, as in Latin it is called *curia*. Therefore in genuine German, in our mother tongue, it ought to be called a Christian congregation or assembly [*eine christliche Gemeinde oder Sammlung*], or, best of all and most clearly, holy Christendom [*eine heilige Christenheit*].

So also the word *communio*, which is added, ought to be rendered not "communion" [*Gemeinschaft*] but "congregation" [*Gemeinde*]. And it is nothing else than an interpretation or explanation by which someone meant to explain what the Christian church is. This our people, who understood neither Latin nor German, have rendered "communion of saints" [*Gemeinschaft der Heiligen*], although no German language speaks thus nor understands it thus. But to speak correct German, it ought to be "a congregation of saints" [*eine Gemeinde der Heiligen*]—that is, a congregation made up purely of saints—or, to speak yet more plainly, "a holy congregation" [*eine heilige Gemeinde*]. I say this in order that the words "communion of saints" [*Gemeinschaft der Heiligen*] may be understood, because the expression has become so established by custom that it cannot well be eradicated, and it is treated almost as heresy if one should attempt to change a word.

But this is the meaning and substance of this addition: I believe that there is on earth a little holy group and congregation of pure saints under one head, even Christ, called together by the Holy Spirit in one faith, one mind and understanding, with manifold gifts, yet agreeing in love, without sects or schisms. I am also a part and member of the same, a sharer and joint owner of all the goods it possesses, brought to it and incorporated into it by the Holy Spirit by having heard and continuing to hear the Word of God, which is the beginning of entering it. For formerly, before we had attained to this, we were altogether of the devil, knowing nothing of God and of Christ. Thus, until the last day, the Holy Spirit abides with the holy congregation or Christendom by means of which he fetches us to Christ and which he employs to teach and preach to us the Word, whereby he works and promotes sanctification, causing it [this community] daily to grow and become strong in the faith and its fruits that he produces.

We further believe that in this Christian church we have forgiveness of sin, which is wrought through the holy sacraments and absolution, as well as through all manner of consolatory promises of the entire gospel. Therefore whatever is to be preached concerning the sacraments belongs here, and in short the whole gospel and all the official responsibilities of Christianity, which also must be preached and taught without ceasing. For although the grace of God is secured through Christ, and sanctification is wrought by the Holy Spirit through the Word of God in the unity of the Christian church, yet on account of our flesh that we bear about with us we are never without sin.

Everything, therefore, in the Christian church is ordered to the end that we shall daily obtain there nothing but the forgiveness of sin through the Word and signs to comfort and encourage our consciences as long as we live here. Thus, although we have sins, the [grace of the] Holy Spirit does not allow them to injure us, because we are in the Christian church, where there is nothing but [continuous, uninterrupted] forgiveness of sin, both in that God forgives us and in that we forgive, bear with, and help each other.

But outside of this Christian church, where the gospel is not, there is no forgiveness, as also there can be no holiness [sanctification]. Therefore all who seek and wish to merit holiness [sanctification] not through the gospel and forgiveness of sin but by their works have expelled and severed themselves [from this church].

Meanwhile, however, while sanctification has begun and is growing daily, we expect that our flesh will be destroyed and buried with all its uncleanness and will come forth gloriously and arise to entire and perfect holiness in a new eternal life. For now we are only half pure and holy, so that the Holy Spirit has ever [some reason why] to continue his work in us through the Word and daily to dispense forgiveness until we attain to that life where there will be no more forgiveness but only perfectly pure and holy people, full of godliness and righteousness, removed and free from sin, death, and all evil, in a new, immortal, and glorified body.

Behold, all this is to be the office and work of the Holy Spirit, that he begin and daily increase holiness on earth by means of these two things, the Christian church and the forgiveness of sin. But in our dissolution he will accomplish it altogether in an instant and will forever preserve us therein by the last two parts.

But the term "resurrection of the flesh" [*Auferstehung des Fleisches*] here employed is not according to good German idiom. For when we Germans hear the word "flesh" [*Fleisch*], we think no further than of a butcher's slaughterhouse. But in good German idiom we would say "resurrection of the body"

[*Auferstehung des Leibes* or *Leichnams*]. However, it is not a matter of much moment if we only understand the words aright.

This, now, is the article that must ever be and remain in operation. For creation we have received; redemption, too, is finished, but the Holy Spirit carries on his work without ceasing to the last day. And for that purpose he has appointed a congregation on earth by which he speaks and does everything. For he has not yet brought together all his Christian church nor dispensed forgiveness. Therefore, we believe in him who through the Word daily brings us into the fellowship of this Christian church and through the same Word and the forgiveness of sins bestows, increases, and strengthens faith, in order that when he has accomplished it all, and we abide therein and die to the world and to all evil, he may finally make us perfectly and forever holy, which now we expect in faith through the Word.

Behold, here you have the entire divine essence, will, and work depicted most exquisitely in quite short and yet rich words, wherein consists all our wisdom, which surpasses and exceeds the wisdom, mind, and reason of all men. For although the whole world with all diligence has endeavored to ascertain what God is, what he has in mind and does, yet it has never been able to attain to [the knowledge and understanding of] any of these things. But here we have everything in richest measure; for here in all three articles he has himself revealed and opened the deepest abyss of his paternal heart and of his pure unutterable love. For he has created us for this very object, that he might redeem and sanctify us; and in addition to giving and imparting to us everything in heaven and on earth, he has given to us even his Son and the Holy Spirit, by whom to bring us to himself. For (as explained above) we could never attain to the knowledge of the grace and favor of the Father except through the Lord

Christ, who is a mirror of the paternal heart, outside of whom we see nothing but an angry and terrible Judge. But of Christ we could know nothing either, unless it had been revealed by the Holy Spirit.

These articles of the Creed, therefore, divide and separate us Christians from all other people on earth. For all outside of Christianity, whether heathen, Turks, Jews, or false Christians and hypocrites, although they believe in and worship only one true God, yet know not what his mind toward them is and cannot expect any love or blessing from him; therefore they abide in eternal wrath and damnation. For they have not the Lord Christ and, besides, are not illumined and favored by any gifts of the Holy Spirit.

From this you perceive that the Creed is a doctrine quite different from the Ten Commandments; for the latter teaches indeed what we ought to do, but the former tells what God does for us and gives to us. Moreover, apart from this, the Ten Commandments are written in the hearts of all men; the Creed, however, no human wisdom can comprehend, but it must be taught by the Holy Spirit alone. The latter doctrine [of the law], therefore, makes no Christian, for the wrath and displeasure of God abide on us still, because we cannot keep what God demands of us; but this [namely, the doctrine of faith] brings pure grace and makes us godly and acceptable to God. For by this knowledge we obtain love and delight in all the commandments of God, because here we see that God gives himself entirely to us, with all that he has and is able to do, to aid and direct us in keeping the Ten Commandments: the Father, all creatures; the Son, his entire work; and the Holy Spirit, all his gifts.

SOLA SCRIPTURA

5

THAT DOCTRINES OF MEN
ARE TO BE REJECTED

In 1521, after having spent several years promoting his reformational ideas in print and public debates, Luther was called to give an account of his efforts before the Holy Roman emperor, Charles V. In this famous confrontation, Luther stated that he would only believe Christian doctrine insofar as it could be proved to him by sound reason or by the Bible. The emperor declared him an outlaw, which meant that anyone could legally kill him after thirty days and not be prosecuted. While Luther was on his way back to his adopted hometown of Wittenberg, his prince, Fredrick the Wise, secretly kidnapped him and took him to Wartburg Castle for his own protection. Luther spent a year there in hiding. It was during this year that he translated the New Testament into German. In 1522 Luther came out of hiding and returned to Wittenberg.

While at the Wartburg Castle, Luther talked with some of his hosts about the importance of the supreme authority of the Bible and about Christian liberty. Once Luther had returned to Wittenberg from the Wartburg Castle, issues related to Christian liberty became very important to people who had joined his movement. Most centrally, people were concerned that in following the principle of Christian liberty they might fall into sin by not obeying the laws established by the medieval church.

It should be understood that in the Middle Ages the Roman Catholic Church developed an elaborate set of church laws. Some of these laws existed as a means of regulating church offices, the rights of the clergy, and what constituted proper and improper marriages. Other laws dealt with what kinds of foods monks and nuns were allowed to eat and the sorts of clothes that they were allowed to wear. Lastly, there were laws dictating what kinds of ritual observances ordinary Christians should obey at different points in the liturgical year. For example, it was considered a sin to eat meat, eggs, and butter at certain points in the liturgical year. It was even considered sacrilegious to have conjugal relations with one's own spouse on certain special holy days. Although none of these laws were in the Bible, many (though not all) theologians claimed that Christ had given the right to the church to mandate certain laws of its own accord, as long as they did not directly conflict with the received interpretation of Scripture.

Luther's answer to those who were afraid to disobey these church laws was to emphasize the ultimate authority of the Bible and the reality of Christian liberty. Christian liberty means that through faith in Christ, Christians are free from the need to earn their salvation. Jesus has already earned our redemption on the cross and, therefore, by trusting in him we gain salvation. As a result, Christians gain freedom from needing to do anything to earn their salvation. Likewise, Christians are also free to obey God and serve their neighbor in the kingdom of the world. They do this by obeying God's commandments as set down in Scripture. They are under no obligation to obey the commandments of the pope or other church officials.

As noted above, many Catholics of Luther's time believed that Christ had given the institutional church the ability to prescribe good works and other ritual actions that would merit salvation. Luther shows in this short treatise that the Reformation principle of "Christ alone" is the natural corollary of "Scripture alone." As he demonstrates, Christ is the Lord of the Scriptures. Moses and the Old Testament prophets prophesied of Christ and he himself authorized the witness of the apostles set down in the New Testament. For this reason, Scripture possesses Christ's own authority and grants Christian liberty in matters of food and dress. The institutional church, or other Christian leaders, cannot by its authority contradict Christ. Christ teaches throughout the Scriptures that Christians are under no obligation to obey meaningless and human-made ritual observances in order to earn their salvation. For this reason, people need not feel guilty when they stop obeying the pope and his human-made laws.

To all who read or hear this little book, may God grant grace and understanding. Amen. I, Martin Luther, have published this brief book for the comfort and saving of the poor consciences that are by the law of men held in bondage in monasteries and convents, that they may be able to arm and strengthen themselves with the Word of God, so as to be steadfast in the pains of death and other trials. But those who are proud and unruly, these I warn that I do not wish my words to help them. This Christian liberty I would have preached only to poor, humble, imprisoned consciences, so that poor children, nuns, and monks who would like to escape from their bondage may inform their consciences how they may do so with God's approval and without danger, and use their freedom in an orderly and Christian way. May God grant his blessing. Amen.

Reasons from Scripture for Rejecting the Doctrine of Men

Moses in Deuteronomy 4:2 says, "You shall not add to the word that I command you, nor take from it, that you may keep the commandments of the LORD your God that I command you." But someone will say that Moses speaks only of his word; but to the books of Moses there have also been added many books of the prophets and the entire New Testament. I answer: True; but nothing new has been added. The same things that are found in the books of Moses are found in the others. It is indeed stated in different words and the histories are different, but throughout [Scripture] there is one and the same teaching.

For it is beyond question that all the Scriptures point to Christ alone. Now Christ says, in John 5:46, "Moses . . . wrote of me." Therefore everything that is in the other books is also in the books of Moses, and these are the original documents (Isa. 29:13) that the Lord quotes in Matthew 15:8–9: "This people honors me with their lips, but their heart is far from me; in vain do they worship, teaching as doctrines the commandments of men." On his word we must build in all things rather than on all angels and creatures (Gal. 1:8). The same Christ in the same chapter, Matthew 15:11, says, "It is not what goes into the mouth that defiles a person, but what comes out of the mouth; this defiles a person."

This saying and judgment must be well understood, for it is powerful and mightily overthrows all teaching, custom, and way of life that distinguishes between foods. It sets all consciences free from all laws concerning food and drink, so that it is allowable to eat milk, butter, eggs, cheese, and meat every day, whether it be Sunday or Friday, Lent or Advent, and no one needs to pay butter-money or buy butter-letters.[1] For this word stands firm and does not deceive: "It is not what goes into the mouth that defiles a person."

From this it follows, first, that it is a lie when they say that St. Peter instituted the fast days and that the commandment of the church has made it a mortal sin to eat eggs, butter, milk, and meat on fast days. For neither St. Peter nor the church

1. These are certificates that allowed medieval Christians the right to buy and eat butter during seasons of the liturgical years where the Roman Catholic Church had banned the use of butter for penitential purposes.

institutes or teaches anything contrary to Christ. And if they did, we must not obey them. Not that it would be wicked to abstain from this practice. But it is wicked to make a requirement and a commandment of that which is free and to pretend that something defiles and is sin of which Christ himself says that it is no sin and does not defile.

Secondly, it follows that for the pope to sell letters and grant permission to eat butter, meat, and so forth is the devil's wanton mischief. For Christ in this word has already made it a matter of liberty and has permitted it.

In the third place, it is an error and a lie to say that goldfasts, banfasts, and the fasts on the eve of apostles' and saints' days must be observed and that nonobservance is sin because the church has so commanded.[2] For against everything of the kind stands this word of Christ: "It is not what goes into the mouth that defiles a person." Fasting should be free and voluntary, both as to the day and as to the food, forever.

Fourthly, the orders of St. Benedict and of St. Bernard, the Carthusians,[3] and all others that avoid the use of meat and other food because they hold that this is necessary and commanded and that not to do so would be sin, contradict Christ. For their law flatly contradicts the word of Christ that says, "It is not what goes into the mouth that defiles a person." Then they must make Christ a liar when he says, "It is not what goes into the mouth that defiles a person." Thus you see that this one saying of Christ mightily condemns all orders and spiritual rules.[4] For

2. These are fasts that the medieval Roman Catholic Church demanded of ordinary Christians. Observing these rules was meant to help Christians merit their salvation.

3. These are monastic organizations popular in the Middle Ages. People believed that by living a life of self-denial they could more easily follow Christ and merit their salvation.

4. In other words, being a monk and following a monastic rule (that is, a set of rules that prescribe what a monk can and cannot do in order to earn his salvation) is contrary to the command of Jesus.

if it is not what goes into the mouth that defiles a person, how much less will that defile which is put on the body? Whether it be a monk's hooded robe, coat, shirt, hose, shoes, cloak, whether green, yellow, blue, red, white, motley,[5] or whatever one wish. And the same is true of places, whether churches, cells, or the rooms of a house.

It follows that he who regards it a sin for a monk to go without the dress of his order and would not leave it a matter of freedom also makes Christ a liar and makes that a sin which Christ freed from sin, and says "Yes!" where Christ has said "No!" What then are such monks but people who say to Christ's very face, "You lie! There is sin in that which you say there is no sin!" It will not help them to quote St. Bernard, St. Gregory, St. Francis, and other saints. We must hear what Christ says, who alone has been made our teacher by the Father, when on Mount Tabor he said, in Matthew 17:5, "This is my beloved Son, with whom I am well pleased; listen to him." He did not say, Hear you St. Bernard, St. Gregory, etc., but, Hear him, him, him, my beloved Son. Who knows how much the saints sinned or did right in this matter? What they did, they did not do of necessity nor by commandment. Or if they did it as of necessity and by commandment, they were mistaken, and we must not forsake Christ to follow them. All this is confirmed by Christ in the words that follow in Matthew 15:18–20: "But what comes out of the mouth proceeds from the heart, and this defiles a person. For out of the heart come evil thoughts, murder, adultery, sexual immorality, theft, false witness, slander. These are what defile a person."

Here we ask: If that alone is sin and defiles a man, which proceeds from the heart, as Christ here so strongly argues and

5. "Motley" refers to a jester's costume.

decides, how then can butter, milk, eggs, or cheese defile, which proceed not from the mouth nor from the heart, but come from the bellies of cows and of hens? Who has ever seen meat, tonsures, monk's robes, monasteries, or hair shirts coming out of men's mouths? Then it must be the cows that sin in giving us milk and butter, and in bearing calves!

Therefore, all the laws of monks and of men concerning food, clothing, and places and all things that are external are not only blasphemy of God and lying and deceiving but the buffoonery of apes. It is true, a man may have an inordinate desire to eat excessively and to dress extravagantly, but that proceeds from the heart and may refer to fish as well as to meat, to gray homespun as well as to red velvet. In short, Christ does not lie when he says, "That which goes into the mouth does not defile a man, but that which comes out of the mouth, this defiles a man."

But if it is true that neglect to do what men command neither defiles nor is sin, then on the other hand, the keeping and doing of men's commandments cannot make us clean nor give us merit; since only the opposite of sin and of the unclean is clean and gives merit. Therefore, all of the monastic life neither makes clean nor produces merit. And that is what the Lord Christ means when he says in Matthew 15:9, "In vain do they worship me, teaching as doctrines the commandments of men." Why "in vain"? Because neglecting them is no sin and keeping them is no merit, but both are free.

They therefore deceive themselves and make meritorious of that which is no merit and are afraid of sinning where there is no sin. As Psalm 14:5 says, "There have they trembled for fear, where there was no fear."[6] St. Paul in 1 Timothy 4:1–7 says,

---

6. This version of the text is not in the original Hebrew but only in the Latin translation of the Bible used in the Middle Ages called the Vulgate. Luther would have been more familiar with it at this point in his career than the original text.

Now the Spirit expressly says that in later times some will depart from the faith by devoting themselves to deceitful spirits and teachings of demons, through the insincerity of liars whose consciences are seared, who forbid marriage and require abstinence from foods that God created to be received with thanksgiving by those who believe and know the truth. For everything created by God is good, and nothing is to be rejected if it is received with thanksgiving, for it is made holy by the word of God and prayer.

If you put these things before the brothers, you will be a good servant of Christ Jesus, being trained in the words of the faith and of the good doctrine that you have followed. Have nothing to do with irreverent, silly myths. Rather train yourself for godliness.

Oh, how this thunders and storms against all the works, doctrines, and orders of mere humans! First, if they brag that they have taken their practice from the pope and from holy fathers,[7] what will Christ's judgment be? Will he not say, "Paul, my apostle, is my chosen instrument," as Luke writes in Acts 9:15. "Why then have you not ascribed greater authority to his word than to that of the pope and the fathers, of whom you do not know whose instrument they are?"

Next, we ask them whether butter, eggs, meat, milk, and all the food that they avoid on fast days and in the orders have not been created by God and are not God's good creatures? Then it is certain that they are the men of whom Paul here says that they prohibit the food that God has created and has given to believers to use. And they also prohibit marriage so that they cannot escape: this passage fits them and is spoken of them. Let us see what Paul thinks of them and how he reprimands them:

7. "Holy fathers" refers to the theologians of the early church.

1. They have deviated from the faith. For they could not have introduced such doctrines and works if they had not thought the doctrines and works would make them pious and save them. But such an opinion is of itself a sure sign that they have fallen away from the faith, since it is the work of faith alone to do that which they expect works to do, as has frequently been said.

2. They give heed to seducing spirits. He does not say "to seducing men," but "to seducing spirits"; and these are they who pretend to be spiritual and bear the name spiritual and claim to be of the Spirit and in the Spirit. But since they are without faith, it is impossible for them not to be mistaken in spiritual matters. Hence this is a fitting succession: they depart from the faith and follow after error in the spirit.

3. Their doctrines he calls "doctrines of devils." This also must follow where faith and the true Spirit are wanting. The devil gives them the seducing spirit and leads them on with beautifully varnished doctrines and works, so that they think they are altogether spiritual. But since the doctrine does not originate in the Scriptures, it can be the doctrine of no one but the devil.

4. They speak lies. For they at times quote even the Scriptures and the sayings of the fathers and use them to support their doctrines, as we see them do daily. But this is all false and a lie, since the Scriptures are altogether against them.

5. It is sheer hypocrisy. This is true and needs no comment. For all that they do is only appearance and show, concerned with external matters of food and clothes.

6. They have their conscience burned with a hot iron; that is, they have an unnatural conscience. For where there is no sin nor matter of conscience, they make sin and a matter of conscience, as was said above, just as a scar caused by burning is an unnatural mark on the body.

7. They prohibit marriage by creating a way of life in which there shall be no marriage, as we see in the case of both priests and monks. Wherefore, behold the judgment of God on such doctrines and way of life: that they are doctrines of devils, seducing doctrines, false doctrines, faithless doctrines, hypocritical doctrines. God help us! What would it help you if you had made a thousand vows and oaths on such doctrines? No, the stricter the vow, the more reason to break it, because it was made after the devil's doctrines and against God.

But see how cleverly they worm themselves out and ward off this text from themselves, saying that it does not apply to them but to the Tatianists, the heretics who condemned marriage altogether.[8] Paul, however, does not speak here of those who condemn marriage but of those who forbid it for the sake of appearing spiritual. He who forbids marriage is the devil's disciple and apostle, as the words clearly say. And since the pope does this, he must be the devil's disciple, as must all his followers; otherwise, St. Paul must be a liar.

8. They forbid the food that God has created. Here, again, you see that the doctrines of man are ascribed to the devil by God himself through the mouth of Paul. What greater and more terrible thing would you wish to hear concerning the doctrines of men than that they are a falling away from the faith, seducing, false, devilish, and hypocritical? But if the doctrine that forbids certain kinds of food is devilish and unchristian, that which concerns clothes, tonsures,[9] places, and everything external will be just as devilish and unchristian.

8. Luther is referring to a group of early Christian heretics who followed an Assyrian theologian named Tatian. They condemned and rejected all sexual union, along with material reality in general.

9. This is a kind of hairstyle worn by monks in which the crown of the head is shaved.

But here again they worm themselves out and say that St. Paul is speaking of the Manicheans.[10] St. Paul speaks of the forbidding of meats, and be they Manicheans or Tatianists, the pope and his followers forbid meats. Paul speaks of the work that we see that the pope does. Therefore we cannot save him from this text. If some other man arose today or tomorrow and forbade meats, would it not apply to him, even if he were no Manichean? If that way of interpreting Scripture were true, we might boldly do what Paul here forbids, and say, "It does not apply to us, but to the ancient Manicheans." But that is not the way. Whether the pope with his monks and priests are or are not Manichean, I do not discuss. But I do say, that in [the pope's] teaching and works he contradicts the teaching of St. Paul more than any Manichean.

9. They are unthankful. For God has created meats, says St. Paul, to be received with thanksgiving. And they refuse to receive them that they may have no occasion to be thankful for God's goodness. The reason for which is that they have no faith and do not know the truth. For Paul says in 1 Timothy 4[:4], "For everything created by God is good, and nothing is to be rejected if it is received with thanksgiving."

10. Paul rebukes them as wicked, harmful preachers; for he says that Timothy shall be a good preacher, nourished up in the words of faith and of good doctrine, if he will remind the brethren of these things. It follows that they who teach the contrary must be wicked preachers and be nourished with words of unbelief and of wicked doctrines.

11. He calls such doctrines profane and old wives' fables. Is not that foolish talk? He says that the great doctors[11] busy

10. This was a heresy in the early church that taught that matter and darkness were manifestations of an evil principle that was equal to and at war with a good principle of light and spirit.

11. Luther uses the term "doctors" to refer to theologians of the church.

themselves with fables such as old wives chatter about behind
the stove and calls them profane, unchristian, and unholy idle
talk, although the doctors claim that they are the very essence
of holiness! Who has ever heard the doctrines of men so terribly
decried in every way? [It is said] that they are apostate, unbelieving, unchristian, heathen, seducing, devilish, false, hypocritical,
searing the conscience, unthankful, that they dishonor God and
his creature and are harmful fables and old wives' chatter. Let
him who can, flee from beneath this judgment of God. St. Paul
in Colossians 2:16 and the following verses [through v. 23] says,

> Therefore let no one pass judgment on you in questions of food
> and drink, or with regard to a festival or a new moon or a Sab-
> bath. These are a shadow of the things to come, but the sub-
> stance belongs to Christ. Let no one disqualify you, insisting
> on asceticism and worship of angels, going on in detail about
> visions, puffed up without reason by his sensuous mind, and not
> holding fast to the Head, from whom the whole body, nourished
> and knit together through its joints and ligaments, grows with
> a growth that is from God.
>
> If with Christ you died to the elemental spirits of the world,
> why, as if you were still alive in the world, do you submit to
> regulations—"Do not handle, Do not taste, Do not touch"
> (referring to things that all perish as they are used)—according
> to human precepts and teachings? These have indeed an appear-
> ance of wisdom in promoting self-made religion and asceticism
> and severity to the body, but they are of no value in stopping
> the indulgence of the flesh.

Is St. Paul here also speaking of the Manicheans or Tatianists?
Or can we find excuse here for the papists?[12] He speaks against

---

12. By "papist" Luther means those who continued to adhere to the papacy and the
theology of the medieval Western church. This group of people have come to be called
"Roman Catholics" in the modern world.

those who take captive the consciences of men with the doctrines of men and make matters of conscience of food, drink, clothes, days, and everything that is external. And it cannot be denied that the pope, the chapters, and the monasteries with their rules and statutes do this when they forbid the eating of meat, eggs, and butter and the wearing of ordinary clothes such as other people wear.

And here stands St. Paul, who says, (1) "Let no man burden your consciences, or judge or condemn you in respect of food, drink, clothes, or days." What does that mean if not this: Do not be priests or monks, nor in any way keep the pope's laws, and do not believe him when he says that a certain thing is sin or a matter of conscience.

See, here God through Paul commands us to despise the laws of the pope and of the monasteries and to keep them free so that they do not bind our conscience. That is as much as to say: Do not become monks or priests, and let him who has become monk or priest turn back, or else retain his position as a matter of freedom without constraint of conscience.

And although Paul wrote this of the Jews, who did such things according to the law (for he says in Colossians 2:17 that they have the shadow and type of things to come, but that the body itself is in Christ), yet it holds much more against the decrees of the pope and of the monks. For if that which God has decreed comes to an end and shall no longer bind the consciences of men, how much more should men neither decree nor keep anything that would bind the conscience? And further on more will be said about the laws of mere men, for (2) he says, "Let no one seduce you or lead you toward the prize into a dead end."

What does this mean but to lead men to works and away from faith—which alone is the one right road by which to gain the prize of salvation—to strive toward heaven by other ways, and to claim that this is the way to gain the prize? And this is what the orders and the pope's doctrines do. And what are the ways they propose?

Listen: (3) he says, "asceticism and worship of angels." What words could better fit the orders? Is it not true that the pope and all of them talk a great deal of their obedience, which is said to be the noblest virtue—that is, the precious spiritual humility of the papists? But who has commanded this humility? They themselves have invented it and pursued it that they might seduce themselves. For with it they have withdrawn themselves from the common humility and obedience that God has commanded—namely, that everyone shall humble himself and be subject to his neighbor. But they are subject to no man on earth and have withdrawn themselves entirely; they have made an obedience and a humility of their own after their statutes. Yet they claim that their obedience is superhuman, perfect, and, as if it were, angelic, although there are no more disobedient and less humble people on earth than they are.

In the same way they also have their vows of chastity and poverty. They do not work like other people, but like the angels in heaven, they praise and worship God day and night; in short, their life is heavenly, although nowhere on earth can you find more horrible unchastity, greater wealth, less devoted hearts, or more hardened people than in this spiritual way of life, as everyone knows. Yet they seduce all the world from the true way to the dead end of their self-willed, beautiful, spiritual, and angelic life. All this, it seems to me, is not spoken of the Jews nor of the Manicheans but of the papists; the works prove it.

(4) He [Paul] says, "He walks in such religion and in that which he has never seen." This is the very worst feature of the doctrines of men and the life built on them, that they are without foundation and without any basis in the Scriptures and that

men cannot know whether what they do is good or wicked. For all their life is an uncertain venture. If you ask them whether they are certain that what they are and do is pleasing to God, they say they do not know, they must take the chances: "the end will show us." And this is all they can say, for they have no faith, and faith alone makes us certain that all that we are is well-pleasing to God, not because of our merit but because of his mercy. Therefore, all their humility, obedience, and all of their religion is, at the very best, uncertain and in vain.

(5) "Puffed up without reason"—that is, they have no reason to vainly puff themselves up. For although their practices are uncertain, unbelieving, and altogether damnable, yet they make bold to puff themselves up and to claim that they have the best and the only true way, so that in comparison with theirs every other manner of living stinks and is nothing at all. But this puffed-up carnal mind of theirs they neither see nor feel, so great is their angelic humility and obedience! Oh, the fruit of the doctrines of men!

(6) "Not holding fast to the Head," which is Christ. For the doctrines of men and Christ cannot agree; one must destroy the other. If the conscience finds comfort in Christ, the comfort derived from works and doctrines must fall; if it finds comfort in works, Christ must fall. The heart cannot build on a twofold foundation: one must be forsaken. Now we see that all the comfort of the papists rests on their practices; for if it did not rest on them, they would not respect them and would give them up, or else they would use them as matters of freedom, how and when they pleased. If there were no other misfortune connected with the doctrines of men, this were of itself all too great, that for their sake Christ must be forsaken, the Head must be lost, and the heart must build on such an abomination. For this reason St. Peter calls the orders abominable and damnable heresies that

deny Christ, when he says, in 2 Peter 2:1, "But false prophets also arose among the people, just as there will be false teachers among you, who will secretly bring in destructive heresies, even denying the Master who bought them."

(7) It is clear enough that he means our spiritual way of life when he says, "If with Christ you died to the elemental spirits of the world, why, as if you were still alive in the world, do you submit to regulations—'Do not handle, Do not taste, Do not touch'?" etc. Who can here deny that God through St. Paul forbids us to teach and to hear all doctrines of men, insofar as they constrain the conscience? Who then can with a good conscience be a monk or a priest, or be subject to the pope? They must confess that their consciences are taken captive with such laws. Thus you see what a mighty saying this is against all doctrines of men. It is dreadful to hear that they forsake Christ the Head, deny the faith, and so necessarily become heathen, and yet think that their holiness upholds the world.

(8) Paul, in Galatians 1:8–9, says, "But even if we or an angel from heaven should preach to you a gospel contrary to the one we preached to you, let him be accursed. As we have said before, so now I say again: If anyone is preaching to you a gospel contrary to the one you received, let him be accursed." In these words you hear a judgment of God against the pope and all doctrines of men, which says that they are under the ban. And this ban is not like the pope's ban;[13] it is eternal and separates a man from God, from Christ, from all salvation, and from everything that is good and makes him the companion of devils. Oh, what a terrible judgment this is! Look now, whether the pope, priests, and monks do not proclaim another and a different doctrine

13. By "ban" Luther means expulsion or excommunication from the Roman Catholic Church.

than that taught by Christ and his apostles. We said above that Christ teaches, "It is not what goes into the mouth that defiles a person." Contrary to this and beyond it the pope, priests, and monks say, "Christ, you lie in saying this! For the eating of meat defiles a Carthusian and condemns him, and the same is true of the other orders!" Is not this striking Christ on the mouth, calling him a liar and blaspheming him, and teaching other doctrines than he taught? Therefore it is a just judgment that they in their great holiness are condemned like blasphemers of God with an eternal ban.

(9) Paul, in Titus 1:13–14, says, "Therefore rebuke them sharply, that they may be sound in the faith, not devoting themselves to Jewish myths and the commands of people who turn away from the truth." This is a strong command that we are not at all to regard the commandments of men. Is this not clear enough? And Paul gives his reason: he says they turn men from the truth. For as has been said above, the heart cannot trust in Christ and at the same time in the doctrines or the works of men. Therefore, as soon as a man turns to the doctrines of men, he turns away from the truth and does not regard it. On the other hand, he who finds his comfort in Christ cannot regard the commandments and the works of men. Look now whose ban you should fear most! The pope and his followers cast you far beyond hell if you do not heed their commandments, and Christ commands you not to heed them on pain of his ban. Consider whom you wish to obey!

(10) Second Peter 2:1–3: "But false prophets also arose among the people, just as there will be false teachers among you, who will secretly bring in destructive heresies, even denying the Master who bought them, bringing on themselves swift destruction. And many will follow their sensuality, and because of them the way of truth will be blasphemed. And in their greed they will

exploit you with false words." So then, the [monastic] orders and monasteries are damnable heresies. Why? Because they deny Christ and blaspheme the way of faith. How? Christ says there is no sin and no righteousness in eating, drinking, clothes, places, and works of men; this they condemn and teach and live the opposite—namely, that sin and righteousness are in these things. Hence Christ must be a liar; he must be denied and blasphemed together with his teaching and faith. And they make use of feigned words and make much of their obedience, chastity, and worship; but only through covetousness, that they may exploit us, until they have brought all the wealth of the world into their possession, on the ground that they are the people who by their worship would help every man to heaven. For this reason they are and remain damnable and blasphemous heresies.

(11) Christ says, in Matthew 24:23–26,

> Then if anyone says to you, "Look, here is the Christ!" or "There he is!" do not believe it. For false christs and false prophets will arise and perform great signs and wonders, so as to lead astray, if possible, even the elect. See, I have told you beforehand. So, if they say to you, "Look, he is in the wilderness," do not go out. If they say, "Look, he is in the inner rooms," do not believe it.

Tell me, how then can a monk be saved? He binds his salvation to a place and says, "Here I find Christ. If I did not remain here I should be lost." But Christ says, "No, I am not here." Who will reconcile these two? Therefore, it is clear from this word of Christ that all doctrines that bind the conscience to places are contrary to Christ. And if he does not allow the conscience to be bound to places, neither does he allow it to be bound to meats, clothes, postures, or anything that is external.

There is no doubt then that this passage speaks of the pope and his clergy and that Christ himself releases and sets free all priests and monks in that he condemns all orders and monasteries and says, "Believe not, go not out," etc. He says the same thing also in Luke 17:20–21: "The kingdom of God is not coming in ways that can be observed, nor will they say, 'Look, here it is!' or 'There!' for behold, the kingdom of God is in the midst of [or within] you." Is not this also clear enough? The doctrines of men can command nothing but external things, and since the kingdom of God is not external, both teachers and disciples miss the kingdom and go astray.

Neither will it help them to say that the holy fathers instituted the [monastic] orders. For Christ has already destroyed this argument since he says that the very elect might be misled—that is, they will err, but not remain in their error. How else would it be an exceeding great error if the elect were not misled? Let the teaching and the practice of the saints be what it will, the words of Christ are certain and clear. It is him that we must follow and not the saints, whose teaching and works are uncertain. What he says stands firm: "The kingdom of God is among you and not at a distance, either here or there." Solomon, in Proverbs 30:5–6, says, "Every word of God proves true; he is a shield to those who take refuge in him. Do not add to his words, lest he rebuke you and you be found a liar."

With this I will end for the present; for there is much more in the prophets, especially in Jeremiah, of which I have written in the treatise on confession. Here then Solomon concludes that he is a liar who adds anything to the words of God; for the Word of God alone is to teach us, as Christ says in Matthew 23:8: "But you are not to be called rabbi, for you have one teacher, and you are all brothers." Amen.

6

THE BONDAGE OF THE WILL

Erasmus was a great scholar and satirist at the time of the Reformation. He edited the first edition of the Greek New Testament published in Western Europe in 1516. Before then, the Bible had only been available in a Latin translation called the Vulgate, which contained many errors that had distorted Christian doctrine. Erasmus also edited works of the theologians of the early church and showed the contrast between early Christianity and the institutional church of his day. This led him to write satirical books making fun of the hypocrisy and abuses of power of the late-medieval church.

Early on, Erasmus was very supportive of Luther and his reforming efforts. But later, Erasmus increasingly did not like what Luther was saying. In promoting the Reformation, Luther was mainly interested in emphasizing that Christianity is about Jesus and the salvation he offers. Although Christians should do good works, they need not do them to earn salvation. Rather, they must rely on Jesus and his work on the cross.

By contrast, Erasmus thought that it was not as important to emphasize Jesus and his work of redemption. Rather, what was more important was to emphasize that Christian people should be good and try to contribute a little bit to their salvation. Erasmus taught this because he thought that the Bible itself was ambiguous as to whether people contributed to earning their salvation or whether Christ was the sole cause of their salvation. In light of this, Erasmus thought it was better to tell people that salvation depends mainly on their own moral efforts in order to prompt them to live an upright life. However, in contrast to contemporary defenders of the pope, Erasmus thought that this good behavior should conform exclusively to the moral teachings of Jesus and not involve the meaningless rituals taught by the medieval church.

Against this, Luther taught that the Bible was clear that Jesus was the sole cause of salvation and not human good works. In this section of his book *The Bondage of the Will* (1525), Luther shows that Scripture is clear in two ways. First, through the simple grammatical meaning of the words, a Christian can come to understand what the Bible teaches on a particular subject. There are obviously some sections of the Bible that are hard to understand. However, this is not because of the subject matter, but rather because we do not know the grammatical meaning of all the words with total certainty. Ultimately, the most important parts of the Bible are grammatically clear, and therefore no doctrinal teaching of the Bible is unclear.

Second and most important, Christ is the center of the Scriptures. His saving death on the cross is the central teaching of the Bible. When this is understood, the whole Scripture opens to the Christian. By working faith in Christ, the Holy Spirit opens the Christian's heart and mind to the central meaning of the whole Bible—namely, that God in Christ saves by grace alone. Just as our salvation is won by grace alone, so too access to our knowledge of that salvation is worked solely by the grace of the Holy Spirit.

The following is a selection from *The Bondage of the Will* in which Luther argues for the clarity of Scripture regarding the gospel of God's grace.

Here you [Erasmus] make a distinction between the Christian dogmas and pretend that some are necessary and some are not necessary. You say that some are obscure and some quite clear. Thus you merely play games with the words of others, or else are trying your hand at rhetorical exercises. And you bring forward, in support of this opinion, that passage of Paul: "Oh, the depth of the riches and wisdom and knowledge of God! How unsearchable are his judgments and how inscrutable his ways!" (Rom. 11:33). And also that of Isaiah: "Who has measured the Spirit of the LORD, or what man shows him his counsel?" (Isa. 40:13).

You could easily say these things, in that you either did not know that you were writing to me [Luther] but for the general public at large, or you did not think that you were writing against me, who, however, I hope you would recognize, has some familiarity with and judgment in the Sacred Letters [the Bible].

This is the distinction that I make (that I also may act like a little rhetorician and logician!): God and the Scripture of God are two things, no less so than God and the creature of God [are two separate things]. That there are in God many hidden things which we do not know, no one doubts, as he [Jesus] himself says concerning the last day, "But concerning the day and hour no one knows . . . but the Father only" (Matt. 24:36). And, "It is not for you to know times or seasons" (Acts 1:7). And again, "I know whom I have chosen" (John 13:18). And Paul, "The Lord knows those who are his" (2 Tim. 2:19). And the like. But that there are in the Scriptures some things opaque and that all things are not quite clear is a report spread abroad by the ungodly Sophists[1] by whose mouth you speak here, Erasmus. But they never have produced, nor ever can produce, one article

---

1. This is Luther's term for the medieval theologians. In ancient Greece, the opponents of Socrates and Plato were named "Sophists." They were known for proving their claims by twisting words rather than using reason. Luther is saying the same thing about the medieval Catholic theologians.

whereby to prove this insane idea of theirs. And it is with such masks that Satan has frightened away men from reading the Sacred Letters.

I do agree that there are many places in the Scriptures obscure and opaque. But not from the majesty of the thing but from our ignorance of certain terms and grammatical particulars, which do not prevent a knowledge of all the things in the Scriptures. For what thing of more importance can remain hidden in the Scriptures now that the seals are broken, the stone rolled from the door of the tomb, and that greatest of all mysteries brought to light, Christ made man: that God is Trinity and unity, that Christ suffered for us and will reign to all eternity? Are not these things known and proclaimed even in our streets?

All the things, therefore, contained in the Scriptures are made manifest; although some places, from the words not being understood, are yet obscure. But to know that all things in the Scriptures are set in the clearest light and then, because a few words are obscure, to report that the things are obscure is absurd and impious. And, if the words are obscure in one place, yet they are clear in another. Now, therefore, it does not matter if the thing is in the light, whether any certain representations of them are obscure or not, if at the same time many other representations of the same thing are in the light.

Therefore, what you infer about the darkness of the Corycian cave[2] is irrelevant, since things are not like this in the Scriptures. For those things that are of the greatest majesty and the most obscure mysteries are no longer in the dark corner but before the very doors, indeed, brought forth and manifested openly!

2. In the time of ancient Greece and Rome, this was a cave that was very dark and thought to be a gate to the underworld. Erasmus used this image as a way of saying that the Bible is very obscure, but in its obscurity it gave people a sense of the terrifying majesty of God.

For Christ has opened our understanding to understand the Scriptures (Luke 24:45). And the gospel is preached to every creature (Mark 16:15; Col. 1:23). "Their voice goes out through all the earth, and their words to the end of the world" (Ps. 19:4). And "whatever was written in former days was written for our instruction" (Rom. 15:4). And again, "All Scripture is breathed out by God and profitable for teaching" (2 Tim. 3:16). Therefore come forward, you and all the Sophists together, and produce any one mystery that remains opaque in the Scriptures!

But if many things still remain opaque to many, this does not arise from obscurity in the Scriptures but from their own blindness or lack of understanding who do not make the effort to look at the perfect clearness of the truth. As Paul says about the Jews in 2 Corinthians 3:15, "A veil lies over their hearts." And again, "And even if our gospel is veiled, it is veiled to those who are perishing. In their case the god of this world has blinded the minds of the unbelievers" (2 Cor. 4:3–4). With the same rashness anyone may cover his own eyes, or go from the light into the dark and hide himself, and then blame the day and the sun for being obscure. Let, therefore, wretched men cease to impute with blasphemous perverseness the darkness and obscurity of their own heart to the completely clear Scriptures of God.

You [Erasmus], therefore, when you quote Paul, saying, "His judgments are incomprehensible," seem to make the pronoun "his" refer to "Scripture." Whereas Paul does not say "The judgments of the Scripture are incomprehensible" but the "judgments of God." Similarly, Isaiah 40:13 does not say "Who has known the mind of the Scripture" but who has known "the mind of the Lord." Although Paul asserts that the mind of the Lord is known to Christians—that is, those things that are freely given unto us—as he says also in the same place, 1 Corinthians 2:10, 16. You see, therefore, how inattentively you have looked over these passages of the Scripture, and you cite them just as aptly as you cite nearly all the passages in defense of free will.

Similarly, your examples that you add, not without suspicion and bitterness, are irrelevant. Such are those concerning the distinction of persons [of the Trinity], the union of the divine and human natures [in Christ], and the unpardonable sin, the ambiguity of all of these being unsatisfactorily demonstrated by you. If you mean the questions of Sophists that have been agitated about concerning these subjects[, then I ask]: What has the completely innocent Scripture done to you that you attribute the abuse of the wickedest of men to its purity? The Scripture simply confesses the Trinity of God, the humanity of Christ, and the unpardonable sin. There is nothing here of obscurity or ambiguity. But how these things are, the Scripture does not say, nor is it necessary to be known. The Sophists employ their dreams here [in these speculative questions]. Attack and condemn them and acquit the Scripture. But if you mean the reality of the matter, I say again, do not attack the Scriptures but the Arians[3] and those to whom the gospel is hid that, through the working of Satan, they might not see the fully clear testimonies concerning the Trinity of the Godhead and the humanity of Christ.

To put it briefly: The clarity of the Scripture is twofold, just as the obscurity is also twofold. The one is external, placed in the ministry of the Word; the other internal, placed in the understanding of the heart. If you speak of the internal clearness, no man sees one iota in the Scriptures but he that has the Spirit of God. All have a darkened heart so that, even if they know how to speak of and set forth all things in the Scripture, yet they

3. The Arians were early Christian heretics who followed the priest Arius. They taught that the Second Person of the Trinity was created by God the Father as a mediator between himself and the created world. They were condemned at the Council of Nicaea in AD 324.

cannot feel them nor know them. Neither do they believe that they are the creatures of God, or anything else according to that of Psalm 14:1: "The fool says in his heart, 'There is no God.'" For the Spirit is necessary to understand the whole of the Scripture and every part of it. If you speak of the external clearness, nothing at all is left obscure or ambiguous. But all things that are in the Scriptures are by the Word brought forth into the clearest light and proclaimed to the whole world.

SOLUS CHRISTUS

7

TRUE AND FALSE VIEWS
OF CHRIST'S SUFFERING

Luther's sermon on "True and False Views of Christ's Suffering" was
written in 1519, only two years after he had posted the *Ninety-Five
Theses*. At this time, Luther was under a great deal of stress due to
the constant personal and theological attacks by the Vatican and its
many supporters. Moreover, the reformer's theology was in a state of
transition from an earlier Roman Catholic–mystical phase to a more
authentic Reformation theology.

Luther's primary audience for this sermon was ordinary Christians who had grown up in the religious culture of the late Middle
Ages. Within that culture, the Good Friday vigil was one of the most
important events of the church year. During this time, Christians were
exhorted to meditate on Christ's sufferings on the cross. In the early
part of this sermon, Luther argues that the Roman Catholic Church
had encouraged people in medieval Europe to think about the events
of Good Friday in several spiritually poisonous ways.

First among these was the use, by many people, of the stories of
the crucifixion as a means of inciting violence against the Jews. Contrary to popular belief, violence against the Jews was something that

the institutional church actually attempted to discourage throughout the Middle Ages. Nevertheless, such violence still occurred (particularly during Lent). Its main source was the belief that contemporary Jews were in some measure responsible for the actions of the tiny minority of Jewish leaders who handed Jesus over to Pilate. Although the reasoning behind this belief was utterly incoherent, vicious, and immoral, it was nevertheless very popular.

Next, popular medieval piety not infrequently involved what might be characterized as a rather unhealthy fixation on the goriness of Christ's sufferings. This was often accompanied by a sense of sorrow for the fact that Christ had to suffer as much as he did. Such piety became especially important during and after the Black Death in the mid-fourteenth century. In the artwork of this period, Mary is pictured as fainting or overwhelmed by distress at the foot of the cross. In a sense, Mary is viewed as suffering along with her son on the cross by means of her sympathy with his state of torment. This gave people who had lost their loved ones in the Black Death a religious figure with whom they could easily identify. However, it also caused people to focus on their sympathy for Christ (or Mary), rather than the saving nature of the work of the cross.

Lastly, there were various superstitious attempts to harness the cross and its power. That is to say, people sought to make the cross a means of personal gain and/or protection from danger. Luther mentions a number of these superstitious practices—notably, covering one's self with crucifixes and various other amulets. Likewise (although he does not mention them), many relics associated with the crucifixion (such as supposed pieces of the true cross) were objects of adoration and pilgrimage.

According to Luther, all these ways of meditating on the cross fail because they essentially misinterpret the cross of Christ. If one follows the New Testament, we will come to recognize that the cross is actually a revelation of the depth of human sin and the depth of divine love. As Luther shows in this sermon, looking to the cross we see that Christ took on himself all our sins. Indeed, everything that happened to him should have happened to us, and from this we can see what our sins truly merited. This is all the more horrifying when we realize that Christ is God and that we have killed God himself with our sins. For this reason, popular hatred of the Jews was in no way justified, because although Christ was killed as a result of the collaboration of some Jewish leaders, they were merely instruments of God's wrath against our sin. Ultimately, heaping blame on the Jews for the crucifixion is merely a distraction from the fact that it is actually we who have killed Christ with our sins.

Recognizing the depth of our sin in the cross itself, we are prepared for the revelation of divine love. Christ is true God and true man and has suffered for us on the cross. This fact shows us how deep God's love actually is. Through the preaching of the cross, God not only works repentance but also faith in the gospel of his grace. Jesus reveals that our sin has been remitted due to his substitutionary sufferings and that he loves us as our Savior. This elicits trust and love for God as a faithful Redeemer. As a result, we will desire to obey God's commandments and mortify sin insofar as it still dwells within us.

In the first place, some people meditate on the sufferings of Christ in a way that they become angry with the Jews. They are satisfied by singing and lamenting about poor Judas. In a similar manner, they complain of other persons and condemn and reproach their enemies. Such an exercise may truly be called a meditation not on the sufferings of Christ but on the wickedness of Judas and the Jews.

In the second place, others have pointed out the different benefits and fruits springing from a consideration of Christ's Passion. Here the saying ascribed to Albertus[1] is misleading, that to think once superficially on the sufferings of Christ is better than to fast a whole year or to pray the Psalter every day. The people thus blindly follow him and act contrary to the true

1. Luther refers to Albertus Magnus, the thirteenth-century theologian who was the teacher of St. Thomas Aquinas.

fruits of Christ's Passion. For they seek therein their own selfish interests. Therefore they decorate themselves with pictures and booklets, with letters and crucifixes, and some go so far as to imagine that they thus protect themselves against the perils of water, fire, sword, and all other dangers. In this way the [purpose of the] sufferings of Christ is to immunize them from suffering, which is contrary to its [true] nature and character.

A third class so sympathize with Christ as to weep and lament for him because he was so innocent, [much] like the women who followed Christ from Jerusalem whom he rebuked in that they should better weep for themselves and for their children. These are those who run away from the Passion season, and are greatly benefited by the departure of Christ from Bethany and by the pains and sorrows of the Virgin Mary, but they never get further. Hence they postpone the Passion for many hours, and God only knows whether it is devised more for sleeping than for watching.

And among these fanatics are those who taught what great blessings come from the holy Mass, and in their simple way they think it is enough if they attend Mass.[2] To this we are led through the sayings of certain teachers [to believe] that the Mass *opere operati, non opere operantis*[3] is acceptable of itself, even without our merit and worthiness, just as if that were enough. Nevertheless the Mass was not instituted for the sake of its own worthiness but for the purpose of meditating on the sufferings of Christ. For where this is not done, we make an unfruitful work out of the Mass, however good it may be in itself. For what

2. It was commonly believed in the popular Christianity of the Middle Ages that merely seeing a Mass (that is, the celebration of the Lord's Supper) performed was meritorious.
3. This Latin phrase roughly translates into "from the work worked, not from the work of the doer." It refers to the Roman Catholic idea that the sacraments work by virtue of simply being performed. Believers need do nothing else other than avoid placing spiritual barriers to their efficacy, such as being in a state of mortal sin.

help is it to you that God is God if he is not God for you? What benefit is it that eating and drinking are in themselves healthful and good if they are not healthful for you, and there is fear that we never become better by reason of our many Masses if we fail to seek the true fruit in them?

Fourth, they meditate on the Passion of Christ correctly who look at Christ in such a manner as to become terrified in their hearts at the sight, and their consciences at once sink in despair. This sense of terror should come about so that you see the severe wrath and the unchangeable seriousness of God in regard to sin and sinners. Indeed, he was unwilling that his only and dearly beloved Son should set sinners free unless he paid the costly ransom for them, as is mentioned in Isaiah 53:8: "He was . . . stricken for the transgression of my people." What happens to the sinner when the dear child is in this manner stricken? A seriousness [regarding sin] must be present that is inexpressible and unbearable, which a person so immeasurably great goes to meet and suffers and dies for it. And, moreover, if you reflect on it deeply that God's Son, the eternal wisdom of the Father, himself suffers, you will indeed experience a sense of terror, and the more you reflect, the deeper the impression will become.

Fifth, that you deeply believe and never doubt in the least that you are the one who thus martyred Christ. For your sins most surely did this thing. Thus St. Peter struck and terrified the Jews as with a thunderbolt in Acts 2:36–37, when he spoke to them all in common, "Jesus whom you crucified," so that three thousand were stricken with terror the same day and tremblingly cried to the apostles: "Brothers, what shall we do?" Therefore, when you view the nails piercing through his hands, firmly believe it is your work. Do you see his crown of thorns? Believe the thorns are your wicked thoughts!

Sixth, therefore see, where one thorn pierces Christ, there more than a thousand thorns should pierce you; indeed, they should eternally even more painfully pierce you. Where one nail is driven through his hands and feet, you should eternally suffer this and even more painful nails, as will be also visited on those who let Christ's sufferings be lost and fruitless as far as they are concerned. For this truthful mirror, Christ, will neither deceive nor mock. For whatever he says must be fully realized.

Seventh, St. Bernard[4] was so terrified by Christ's sufferings that he said, "I imagined I was secure and I knew nothing of the eternal judgment passed on me in heaven, until I saw the eternal Son of God took mercy on me, stepped forward, and offered himself on my behalf in the same judgment. Ah, it does not become me still to play and remain secure when such earnestness is behind those sufferings." Hence he [Jesus] commands the women: "Do not weep for me, but weep for yourselves and for your children" (Luke 23:28), and gives the reason in verse 31: "For if they do these things when the wood is green, what will happen when it is dry?" As if to say: Learn from my martyrdom what you have merited and how you should be rewarded. For here it is true that a little dog was slain in order to terrorize a big one. Likewise the prophet also says that all generations shall lament and bemoan themselves more than him.[5] It is not said they will lament him but rather themselves. Likewise, all were terrified in Acts 2:37, as mentioned before, so that they said to the apostles, "Brothers, what shall we do?" So the church also sings: I will diligently meditate on this, and so my soul within me will exhaust itself.

4. This refers to Bernard of Clairvaux, who was a famous twelfth-century mystic and theologian. Luther frequently quoted Bernard in his early writings, and some newer scholarship (particularly by the Roman Catholic Luther scholar Franz Posset) has connected Luther's Reformation breakthrough to Bernard and his writings.

5. A reference to Jeremiah 4:31.

Eighth, one must skillfully exercise themselves in this matter, for the benefit of Christ's sufferings depends on man coming to a true knowledge of himself, thereby becoming terrified and slain. And where man does not come to this point, the sufferings of Christ are of no true benefit to him. For the characteristic natural impact of Christ's sufferings is that they make all men equal and alike, so that just as Christ was horribly martyred in body and soul for our sins, we must likewise be martyred in our consciences by [the knowledge of] our sins. This takes place not by means of many words but by means of deep thoughts and a profound realization of our sins. Take an illustration: If an evil-doer were judged because he had murdered the child of a prince or king, and you were in safety and sang and played as if you were entirely innocent until one seized you in a horrible manner and convinced you that you had enabled the wicked person to do the act, then you would be in the greatest straits, especially if your conscience also revolted against you. Therefore, how much more anxious you should be when you consider Christ's sufferings. For the evildoers, the Jews, although they have now been judged and banished by God, have still been the servants of your sins, and you are truly the one who strangled and cruci-fied the Son of God through your sins, as has already been said.

Ninth, whoever perceives himself to be so hard and callous that he is not terrified by Christ's sufferings and led to a knowl-edge of self, he should [all the more] fear and tremble. For it cannot be otherwise; you must become conformed to the image and sufferings of Christ, [whether] it is realized in this life or in hell.[6] You must at the time of death, if not sooner, fall into

6. The more accurate Weimar edition of Luther's works actually reads "purgatory" and not "hell." The Lenker translation, which this revised translation is based on, follows the Erlangen edition of Luther's works, which is in turn a revision of the Walch edition. It seems here that later Lutherans, in editing the reformer's work, changed "purgatory"

terror, tremble, quake, and experience all Christ suffered on
the cross. It is truly terrible to be confronted with this on your
deathbed. Therefore you should pray to God to soften your heart
and permit you fruitfully to meditate on Christ's Passion. For
it is impossible for us to meditate profoundly on the sufferings
of Christ by ourselves unless God presses them into our hearts.
Furthermore, neither this meditation nor any other doctrine is
given to you to the end that you should attempt to accomplish
the same goal. Rather, you should first seek and long for the
grace of God, that you may accomplish it through God's grace
and not through your own power. For in this way it happens
that those referred to above never treat the sufferings of Christ
correctly. For they never call on God with that goal in mind
but seek to use their own abilities to achieve it in their own
ways and treat [Christ's] sufferings in a completely human and
fruitless manner.

Tenth, whoever meditates thus on God's sufferings for a day,
an hour, indeed, for a quarter of an hour, we wish to say freely
and publicly that it is better than if he fasts a whole year, prays
the Psalter every day, indeed, than if he hears a hundred Masses.
For such a meditation changes a man's character and almost as
in baptism he is born anew. Then Christ's suffering accomplishes
its true, natural, and noble work: it slays the old Adam, banishes
all lust, pleasure, and security that one may obtain from God's
creatures, just like Christ was forsaken by all, even by God.

Eleventh, since then such a work is not in our hands, it happens that sometimes we pray and do not receive it at the time. In
spite of this, one should not despair or stop praying. At times it
comes when we are not praying for it, in a manner that God wills

---

to "hell." It should be noted that at this point Luther's theology was still in transition
from Roman Catholic to Reformation thought and that he had not yet rejected purgatory as a false doctrine.

and wishes it, for [God's will] must be left free and unbound. Then man is distressed in conscience and is wickedly displeased with his own life. It may easily happen that he does not know that Christ's Passion is working this very thing in him, just like the others meditated on Christ's Passion yet do not gain the true knowledge of self from it. Among the first, the sufferings of Christ are veiled and true, [while] among the others, unreal and false. According to its nature God often reverses things, so that those who do not meditate on the Passion really do meditate on it. [Likewise, often] those who hear the Mass do not hear it, and those who hear it not do hear it.

Twelfth, until the present we have been in the Passion Week and have celebrated Good Friday in the right way: now we come to Easter and Christ's resurrection. When man perceives his sins in this light and is completely terrified in his conscience, he must be on his guard that his sins do not remain in his conscience, for nothing but pure doubt certainly comes out of this. But just as the sins flowed out of Christ and we became conscious of them, so should we pour them again on him and set our conscience free. Therefore see well to it that you act not like perverse people, who bite and devour themselves with their sins in their heart and run here and there with their good works or their own satisfactions[7] or even work themselves out of this condition by means of indulgences[8] and become rid of their sins. This is impossible, and alas, this false refuge of satisfaction and pilgrimages have spread far and wide.

7. This refers to the Roman Catholic sacrament of penance. According to Roman Catholic teaching, although God forgives sins, people must partially make up for the negative effect of sin (temporal punishment) with penitential activities or what are often called "satisfactions."

8. An "indulgence" (which Luther's famous *Ninety-Five Theses* attacked) is the abrogation of the need to make satisfaction by other means. In the late medieval church, this often took the form of pilgrimage or the paying of a fee.

Thirteenth, then cast your sins from yourself and on Christ; believe with a celebratory spirit that your sins are his wounds and sufferings, that he carries them and makes satisfaction for them, as Isaiah 53:6 says: "The LORD has laid on him the iniquity of us all"; and St. Peter in his First Epistle (2:24): "He himself bore our sins in his body on the tree" of the cross; and St. Paul in 2 Corinthians 5:21: "For our sake he made him to be sin who knew no sin, so that in him we might become the righteousness of God." On these and like passages you must rely completely, and so much the more when your conscience torments you. For if you do not take this course but miss the opportunity of stilling your heart, then you will never secure peace and must yet finally despair out of doubt [in your salvation]. For if we deal with the sins in our conscience and let them continue within us and be cherished in our hearts, they become much too strong for us to manage and will live forever. But when we see that they are laid on Christ and he has triumphed over them by his resurrection and we fearlessly believe it, then they are dead and have become as nothing. For on Christ they cannot rest; there they are swallowed up by his resurrection, and you will now see no wound, no pain, in him—that is, no sign of sin. Thus St. Paul speaks in Romans 4:25 that Christ "was delivered up for our trespasses and raised for our justification." That is, in his sufferings he made known our sins and also crucified them; but by his resurrection he makes us righteous and free from all sin if we believe this.

Fourteenth, now if you are not able to believe, then as I said before, you should pray to God for faith. For this is a matter in the hands of God that is entirely free and is at times given openly, while at times secretly, as was just said on the subject of suffering.

Fifteenth, but now exert yourself to this goal. First, do not look at Christ's sufferings any longer; for they have already done their work and terrified you; but press through all difficulties and look to his friendly heart, how full of love it is toward you, which love constrained him to bear the heavy load of your conscience and your sin. As a result, your heart will be loving and sweet toward him, and the assurance of your faith will be strengthened. Then ascend higher through the heart of Christ to the heart of God [the Father], and see that Christ would not have been able to love you if God [the Father] had not willed it in eternal love, to which Christ is obedient in his love toward you. There you will find the divine, good father heart, and as Christ says, through this be drawn to the Father through Christ. Then will you understand the saying of Christ in John 3:16: "For God so loved the world, that he gave his only Son," etc. That means we know God aright if we apprehend him not by his power and wisdom, which terrify us, but by his goodness and love; there our faith and confidence can then stand immovable, and man is truly thus born anew in God.

Sixteenth, when your heart is thus established in Christ and you are an enemy of sin out of love and not out of fear of punishment, Christ's sufferings should also be an example for your whole life, and you should meditate on the same [sufferings] in a different way. Before we have considered Christ's Passion as a sacrament that works in us and which we experience, but now we consider it, [insofar] that we also work, namely thus: if a day of sorrow or sickness weighs you down, think how trifling that is compared with the thorns and nails of Christ. If you must do or leave undone what is distasteful to you, think how Christ was led here and there, bound and a captive. Does pride attack you? See how your Lord was mocked and disgraced with murderers. Do unchastity and lust thrust themselves against you? Think how bitter it was for Christ to have his tender flesh torn, pierced, and beaten again and again. Do hatred and envy war against you, or do you seek vengeance? Remember how Christ with many tears and cries prayed for you and all his enemies, who indeed had more reason to seek revenge. If trouble or whatever adversity of body or soul afflict you, strengthen your heart and say, "Ah, why shouldn't I also suffer a little since my Lord sweat blood in the garden because of anxiety and grief?" It would be a lazy, disgraceful servant who would desire to lie in his bed while his lord was forced to do battle with the pangs of death.

See therefore that one can in this manner find in Christ strength and comfort against all bad behavior and failing. That is the proper observance of Christ's Passion, and that is the fruit of his suffering. And he who exercises himself in this manner does better than by hearing the whole Passion [narrative] or saying all Masses.[9]

And they are called true Christians who incorporate the life and name of Christ into their own life, as St. Paul says in Galatians 5:24: "And those who belong to Christ Jesus have crucified the flesh with its passions and desires." For Christ's Passion must be dealt with not in words and an outward show but in our lives and in truth. Thus St. Paul admonishes us in Hebrews 12:3: "Consider him who endured from sinners such hostility against himself, so that you may not grow weary or fainthearted"; and St. Peter in his First Epistle (4:1): "Since therefore Christ suffered in the flesh, arm yourselves with the same way of thinking."

---

9. The Erlangen edition, which Lenker bases the present translation on, is missing a sentence at this point that is presented in the more accurate Weimar edition. The American edition of *Luther's Works* translates this missing sentence as follows: "This is not to say that Masses are of no value, but they do not help us in such meditations and exercise" (*Luther's Works*, vol. 42, *Devotional Writings 1*, trans. Martin H. Bertram, ed. Martin O. Dietrich [Philadelphia: Fortress, 1971], 14).

8

THE SECOND ARTICLE
OF THE APOSTLES' CREED

Jesus Christ

As was noted earlier, Luther wrote the Small and Large Catechisms in response to the problem of gross ignorance of basic Christian theology among both the common people and the clergy. In writing the catechisms, his aim was in no way to supplant the supreme authority of the Bible but rather to explain its fundamental teachings in order to prepare believers for further study of Scripture and engagement in the life and worship of the church.

In this section of the Large Catechism, Luther discusses the second article of the Apostles' Creed, an early Christian summary of the teachings of Scripture that was used as a confession of faith at the time of baptism. In this particular section, the person and work of Christ are summarized.

There are several important things to recognize in Luther's summary of the person and work of Christ. In terms of his definition of Christ's person, Luther is in complete agreement with the ancient church and its assertion that Jesus Christ is simultaneously true God

125

and true man, born of the Virgin Mary in order to bear the sins of humanity on the cross and rise again. In this, we should observe that although Luther believed Scripture was the supreme authority in all matters of faith and life, he held that the early church's creedal tradition was accurate in its confession of basic scriptural truths (i.e., the Trinity, the person of Christ, etc.). Indeed, Luther claimed that it was only after the strengthening of the papacy in the eleventh century (in fact, a whole new understanding of the role of the pope) that most corruptions had seeped into the church.

Second, it should be noted that in his treatment of the work of Christ, Luther observes that Scripture teaches *both* that Christ died for our sins *and* defeated death and the devil. In this, the reformer combines the emphases of both the ancient and medieval church. Although most early Christian theologians acknowledged that Jesus had died for the sins of humanity, the main accent of their teaching was on the fact that Christ had defeated Satan and saved humanity from the power of death. This is sometimes called the *Christus Victor* model of atonement. By contrast, during the Middle Ages, St. Anselm argued that the most important thing that Jesus had done by his death was to pay the debt of sin that humanity owed God. Most medieval Catholic theologians followed him in this assertion.

In his treatment of Christ's work in this section, Luther shows that the Bible teaches both truths. Jesus is the most supreme Savior because he has saved humanity not only from the debt of sin but also from its negative effects (death, slavery to Satan, etc.). In this, Christ is the perfect Savior of the whole person, both soul and body. Jesus saves the soul (the seat of the moral will) by paying the debt of sin incurred by the soul's perverse moral choices. Jesus saves the body from the degradation and death of our physical life, which Satan brings about as a result of sin.

And in Jesus Christ, his only Son, our Lord, who was conceived by the Holy Spirit, born of the Virgin Mary; suffered under Pontius Pilate, was crucified, dead, and buried; he descended into hell; the third day he rose again from the dead; he ascended into heaven, and sits at the right hand of God the Father Almighty; from there he shall come to judge the living and the dead.

Here we learn to know the Second Person of the Godhead, so that we see what we have from God over and above the temporal goods aforementioned—namely, how he has completely poured forth himself and withheld nothing from us that he has not given us. Now, this article is very rich and broad; but in order to expound it also briefly and in a childlike way, we shall take up one word and sum up in that the entire article—namely (as we have said), that we may here learn how we have been redeemed; and we shall base this on these words [of the Creed]: "In Jesus Christ, our Lord."

If now you are asked, What do you believe in the Second Article of Jesus Christ? answer briefly, I believe that Jesus Christ, true Son of God, has become my Lord. But what is it to become Lord? It is this, that he has redeemed me from sin, from the devil, from death, and [from] all evil. For before I had no Lord nor King but was captive under the power of the devil, condemned to death, enmeshed in sin and blindness.

For when we had been created by God the Father and had received from him all manner of good, the devil came and led us into disobedience, sin, death, and all evil so that we fell under his wrath and displeasure and were doomed to eternal damnation, as we had merited and deserved. There was no counsel, help, or comfort until this only and eternal Son of God in his unfathomable goodness had compassion on our misery and wretchedness and came from heaven to help us. Those tyrants and jailers, then, are all expelled now, and in their place has come Jesus Christ—Lord of life, righteousness, every blessing, and salvation—and has delivered us poor lost men from the jaws of hell, has won us, made us free, and brought us again into the favor and grace of the Father and has taken us as his own property under his shelter and protection that he may govern us by his righteousness, wisdom, power, life, and blessedness.

Let this, then, be the sum of this article that the little word "Lord" signifies simply as much as Redeemer—i.e., he who has brought us from Satan to God, from death to life, from sin to righteousness and who preserves us in the same. But all the points that follow in order in this article serve no other end than to explain and express this redemption, how and whereby it was accomplished—that is, how much it cost him, and what he spent and risked that he might win us and bring us under his dominion; namely, that he became man, [being] conceived and born without [any stain of] sin, of the Holy Spirit and of the Virgin Mary, that he might overcome sin; moreover, that he suffered, died, and was buried, that he might make satisfaction for me and pay what I owe, not with silver nor gold but with his own precious blood. And all this, in order to become my Lord; for he did none of these for himself, nor had he any need of it. And after that he rose again from the dead, swallowed up and devoured death, and finally ascended into heaven and assumed the government at the Father's right hand so that the devil and all powers must be subject to him and lie at his feet until finally, at the last day, he will completely part and separate us from the wicked world, the devil, death, and sin.

9

COMMENTARY ON GALATIANS

Christ Took Our Sin

In this section of the larger Galatians commentary of 1531, Luther discusses Paul's assertion that Christ has become a "curse" for humanity. As Luther observes, going back to St. Jerome, many theologians did not feel that this was an appropriate way of talking about the death of Christ. They followed this line of reasoning: Since God is supremely good, he cannot help but make judgments based on the goodness he sees before him. Therefore, although the New Testament repeatedly asserts that Christ was imputed with the sin of humanity and was made a curse, this cannot be the case. God could not lay the sins of humanity on Christ because Christ was not truly a sinner.

Therefore, according to many of the medieval theologians, all passages in the New Testament teaching that God the Father laid humanity's sin on Christ must be reinterpreted as teaching instead that, in dying, Christ had merited the forgiveness of sins by his obedience to the Father. Since Christ was sinless, he did not need to die, and therefore he performed a superior act of obedience on the cross. According to this view, forgiveness was earned through superior moral behavior (something Catholic theologians refer to as *supererogation*), rather than the result of Christ accepting the punishment due for our sin.

Luther agreed that Christ was righteous in himself and that by his righteous life (culminating in the cross) he had earned justification for those who believe (later Protestant thinkers called this Christ's "active righteousness"). Nevertheless, Luther also insisted that the New Testament clearly taught that Christ had suffered as a curse and bore the sins of humanity (what later Protestant theologians called "passive righteousness"). Ultimately, to be accepted by God, we must be both positively righteous as well as free from the debt of sin. Christ accomplished both of these things on the cross.

Therefore, although Christ was righteous in himself as true God and perfect man, the Father lay all human sin on him. Taking humanity's sin as his own, he paid for it on the cross. In this section of the Galatians commentary, Luther shows not only that this is Paul's teaching but also that if we do not believe our sins have been laid on Christ, then it is up to us to bear them. If we insist on bearing our own sins, this can only result in us being eternally lost.

3:13. Christ redeemed us from the curse of the law by becoming a curse for us—for it is written, "Cursed is everyone who is hanged on a tree."

Jerome and his present-day followers rack their miserable brains over this comforting passage in an effort to save Christ from the supposed insult of being called a curse. They say, "This quotation from Moses does not apply to Christ. Paul is taking liberties with Moses by generalizing the statements in Deuteronomy 21:23. Moses has 'he that is hanged.' Paul puts it 'every one that hanged.' On the other hand, Paul omits the words 'of God' in his quotation from Moses: 'For a hanged man is cursed by God.' Moses speaks of a criminal who is worthy of death." "How," our opponents ask, "can this passage be applied to the holy Christ as if he were cursed by God and worthy to be hanged?" This piece of exegesis may impress the naive as a zealous attempt to defend the honor and glory of Christ. Let us see what Paul has in mind.

Paul does not say that Christ was made a curse for himself. The accent is on the two words "for us." Christ is personally innocent. Personally, he did not deserve to be hanged for any crime of his own doing. But because Christ took the place of others who were sinners, he was hanged like any other transgressor. The law of Moses leaves no loopholes. It says that a transgressor should be hanged. Who are the other sinners? We are. The sentence of death and everlasting damnation had long been pronounced over us. But Christ took all our sins and died for them on the cross. "He poured out his soul to death and was numbered with the transgressors; yet he bore the sin of many, and makes intercession for the transgressors" (Isa. 53:12).

All the prophets of old said that Christ should be the greatest sinner, murderer, adulterer, thief, and blasphemer that ever was or ever could be on earth. When he took the sins of the whole world on himself, Christ was no longer an innocent person. He was a sinner burdened with the sins of a Paul who was a blasphemer, Peter who denied Christ, and David who committed adultery and murder and gave the heathen occasion to laugh at the Lord. In short, Christ was charged with the sins of all men that he should pay for them with his own blood. The curse struck him. The law found him among sinners. He was not only in the company of sinners. He had gone so far as to invest himself with the flesh and blood of sinners. So the law judged and hanged him for a sinner.

In separating Christ from us sinners and holding him up as a holy example, those who promote errors rob us of our best comfort. They misrepresent him as a threatening tyrant who is ready to slaughter us at the slightest provocation.

I am told that it is preposterous and wicked to call the Son of God a cursed sinner. I answer: If you deny that he is a condemned sinner, you are forced to deny that Christ died. It is no less preposterous to say that the Son of God died than to say the Son of God was a sinner. John the Baptist called him "the Lamb of God that takes away the sin of the world." Being the unspotted Lamb of God, Christ was personally innocent. But because he took the sins of the world, his sinlessness was defiled with the sinfulness of the world. Whatever sins I, you, all of us have committed or shall commit, they are Christ's sins as if he had committed them himself. Our sins have to be Christ's sins or we shall perish forever.

Isaiah declares of Christ, "The LORD has laid on him the iniquity of us all" (Isa. 53:6). We have no right to minimize the force of this declaration. God does not amuse himself with words. What a relief for a Christian to know that Christ is covered all over with my sins, your sins, and the sins of the whole world.

The papists[1] invented their own doctrine of faith. They say that [the virtue of] love creates and adorns their faith. By stripping Christ of our sins, by making him sinless, they cast our sins back at us and make Christ absolutely worthless to us. What sort of love is this? If that is a sample of their celebrated love, we want none of it.

Our merciful Father in heaven saw how the law oppressed us and how impossible it was for us to get out from under the

---

1. This is Luther's name for Roman Catholics, since they follow the authority of the pope.

curse of the law. He therefore sent his only Son into the world and said to him, "You are now Peter, the liar; Paul, the persecutor; David, the adulterer; Adam, the disobedient; the thief on the cross. You, my Son, must pay the world's iniquity." The law growls, "All right! If your Son is taking the sin of the world, I see no sins anywhere else but in him. He shall die on the cross." And so therefore the law kills Christ, but we go free.

The argument of the apostle against the righteousness of the law is impregnable. If Christ bears our sins, we do not bear them. But if Christ is innocent of our sins and does not bear them, we must bear them, and we shall die in our sins. "But thanks be to God, who gives us victory through our Lord Jesus Christ" [1 Cor. 15:57].

Let us see how Christ was able to gain the victory over our enemies. The sins of the whole world, past, present, and future, fastened themselves on Christ and condemned him. But because Christ is God, he had an everlasting and unconquerable righteousness. These two, the sin of the world and the righteousness of God, met in a death struggle. Furiously the sin of the world assailed the righteousness of God. Righteousness is immortal and invincible. On the other hand, sin is a mighty tyrant who subdues all men. This tyrant pounces on Christ. But Christ's righteousness is unconquerable. The result is inevitable. Sin is defeated, and righteousness triumphs and reigns forever.

In the same manner was death defeated. Death is emperor of the world. He strikes down kings, princes, all men. He has an idea to destroy all life. But Christ has immortal life, and life immortal gained the victory over death. Through Christ death has lost its sting. Christ is the death of death.

The curse of God waged a similar battle with the eternal mercy of God in Christ. The curse meant to condemn God's mercy. But it could not do it because the mercy of God is everlasting. The curse had to give way. If the mercy of God in Christ had lost out, God himself would have lost out, which, of course, is impossible. "Christ," says Paul, "disarmed the rulers and authorities and put them to open shame, by triumphing over them in him" (Col. 2:15). They cannot harm those who hide in Christ. Sin, death, the wrath of God, hell, the devil are mortified in Christ. Where Christ is near, the powers of evil must keep their distance. St. John says, "And this is the victory that has overcome the world—our faith" (1 John 5:4).

You may now perceive why it is imperative to believe and confess the divinity of Christ. To overcome the sin of a whole world and death and the wrath of God was no work for any creature. The power of sin and death could be broken only by a greater power. God alone could abolish sin, destroy death, and take away the curse of the law. God alone could bring righteousness, life, and mercy to light. In attributing these achievements to Christ, the Scriptures pronounce Christ to be God forever. The article of justification is indeed fundamental. If we remain sound in this one article, we remain sound in all the other articles of the Christian faith. When we teach justification by faith in Christ, we confess at the same time that Christ is God.

I cannot get over the blindness of the pope's theologians, who imagine that the mighty forces of sin, death, and the curse can be vanquished by the righteousness of man's paltry works, by fasting, pilgrimages, Masses, vows, and such outward shows. These blind leaders of the blind turn the poor people over to the mercy of sin, death, and the devil. What chance does a defenseless human creature have against these powers of darkness? They train sinners who are ten times worse than any thief, whore, or murderer. The divine power of God alone can destroy sin and death and create righteousness and life.

When we hear that Christ was made a curse for us, let us believe it with joy and assurance. By faith, Christ changes places with us. He gets our sins; we get his holiness.

By faith alone can we become righteous, for faith invests us with the sinlessness of Christ. The more fully we believe this, the fuller will be our joy. If you believe that sin, death, and the curse are void, why, they are null, zero. Whenever sin and death make you nervous, write it down as an illusion of the devil. There is no sin now, no curse, no death, and no devil because Christ has done away with them. This fact is sure. There is nothing wrong with the fact. The defect lies in our lack of faith.

In the Apostolic Creed we confess, "I believe in the holy Christian church." That means, I believe that there is no sin, no curse, no evil in the church of God. Faith says, "I believe that." But if you want to believe your eyes, you will find many short-comings and offenses in the members of the holy church. You see them succumb to temptation; you see them weak in faith; you see them give into anger, envy, and other evil dispositions. "How can the church be holy?" you ask. It is with the Christian church as it is with the individual Christian. If I examine myself, I find enough unholiness to shock me. But when I look at Christ in me, I find that I am altogether holy. And so it is with the church.

Holy Scripture does not say that Christ was under the curse. It says directly that Christ was made a curse. In 2 Corinthians 5:21 Paul writes, "For our sake he [God] made him [Christ] to be sin who knew no sin, so that in him we might become the righteousness of God." Although this and similar passages may be properly explained by saying that Christ was made a sacrifice for the curse and for sin, yet in my judgment it is better to leave these passages stand as they read: Christ was made sin itself; Christ was made the curse itself. When a sinner gets wise to himself, he does not only feel miserable; he feels like misery personified. He [Christ] does not only feel like a sinner; he feels like sin itself.

To finish with this verse: All evils would have overwhelmed us (as they will overwhelm the unbelievers forever) if Christ had not become the great sinner and guilty bearer of all our sins. The sins of the world got him down for a moment. They came around him like water. In the name of Christ, the Old Testament prophet complained: "Your wrath has swept over me; your dreadful assaults destroy me" (Ps. 88:16). By Christ's salvation we have been delivered from the terrors of God to a life of eternal bliss.

SOLI DEO GLORIA

10

THE FIRST ARTICLE
OF THE APOSTLES' CREED

The Gracious God

As we discussed in an earlier section, Luther wrote the Large Catechism (1529) in response to both the gross immorality and ignorance of the Christian faith among both the parish clergy and the common people. In order to counteract this situation, the reformer sought to give a simple summary of basic biblical teachings. Knowing the basic content of Scripture, people would be better prepared for genuine Christian faith and life as well as for the study of the Scriptures. In this section of the catechism, Luther discusses the first article of the Apostles' Creed, which deals with God the Father and creation.

In discussing the first article of the Apostles' Creed, Luther's emphasis is on the gracious nature of God's decision to create the world and sustain it. In the same way that the second and third articles of the Creed speak of God's gratuitous self-giving through Christ and the Holy Spirit, the first article speaks of God's self-giving through creation. Creation, like justification, is graciously bestowed on those who received it. Creatures do not merit their own creation. They neither exist nor perform good works prior to God calling them into being. Nevertheless, God brings creation into existence out of nothingness through the agency of his Word and Spirit. He does this out of pure grace. Hence, just like salvation, creation comes about solely through grace alone and the Word alone.

Moreover, especially in a fallen world, creatures do not merit their own continued existence through God's sustaining power. Indeed, since human beings are sinful after the fall, they deserve nothing but God's anger and punishment. Nevertheless, in spite of sin and God's consequent holy anger, the Lord still gives all creatures their sustenance and providentially cares for them. He does this because he is a loving God, who loves even when he is not loved in return. For this reason, we should trust and praise God. Although we do not deserve it, he still communicates all good things to us out of his sheer fatherly goodness.

I believe in God the Father Almighty, Maker of heaven and earth.

This [article of the Creed] describes and sets forth most briefly what is the essence, will, activity, and work of God the Father. For since the Ten Commandments have taught us that we are to have only one God, the questions might be asked: "What kind of a person is God? What does he do? How can we praise, or portray and describe him, that he may be known?" Now, this is taught in this and in the following article, so that the Creed is nothing else than the answer and confession of Christians set forth with regard to the first commandment. It is as if you were to ask a little child, "My dear, what kind of a God do you have? What do you know of him?" And he could say, "This is my God: first, [he is] the Father, who has created heaven and earth; besides this only one I regard nothing else as God. For there is no one else who could create heaven and earth."

But for the learned and those who are somewhat advanced [i.e., have acquired some scriptural knowledge], these three articles may all be expanded and divided into as many parts as there are words. But now for young scholars let it suffice to indicate the most important points—namely, as we have said, that this article refers to the creation [and] we [should] emphasize the words "Creator of heaven and earth." But what is the force of this, or what do you mean by these words: "I believe in God, the Father Almighty, Maker, etc."? Answer: This is what I mean and believe, that I am a creature of God—that is, that he has given and constantly preserves to me my body, soul, and life, members great and small, all my senses, reason, and understanding, and so on, food and drink, clothing and support, wife and children, domestics, house and home, etc. Besides, he causes all creatures to serve for the uses and necessities of life sun, moon, and stars in the firmament, day and night, air, fire, water, earth, and whatever it bears and produces, birds and fishes, beasts, grain, and all kinds of produce, and whatever else there is of bodily and temporal goods, good government, peace, security. Thus we learn from this article that none of us has of himself, nor can preserve, his life nor anything that is here enumerated or can be enumerated, however small and unimportant a thing it might be, for all is comprehended in the word "Creator."

Moreover, we also confess that God the Father has not only given us all that we have and see before our eyes but daily preserves and defends us against all evil and misfortune, shields against all sorts of danger and calamity. Moreover, he does all this out of pure love and goodness, without our merit, as a benevolent Father, who cares for us that no evil befall us. But to speak more of this belongs in the other two parts of this article, where we say, "Father Almighty."

Now, since all that we possess (and, beyond this, whatever is in heaven and on the earth) is daily given, preserved, and kept for us by God, it is easily inferred and concluded that it is our duty to love, praise, and thank him for it without ceasing—in short, to serve him with all these things, as he demands and has enjoined in the Ten Commandments.

Here we could say much more if we were to speak at length, how few [people] there are that [actually] believe this article. For we all pass over it, hear it and say it, but neither see nor think about what the words teach us. For if we believed it with [our whole] heart, we would also act accordingly and not walk around so proudly, behave defiantly, and boast as though we had life, riches, power, and honor, etc., of ourselves so that others must fear and serve us. This is the practice of the wretched, perverse world, which is drowned in blindness and abuses all the good things and gifts of God only for its own pride, avarice, lust, and luxury, and never once regards God so as to thank him or acknowledge him as Lord and Creator.

Therefore, this article ought to humble and terrify us all if we believed it. For we sin daily with eyes, ears, hands, body and soul, money and possessions, and with everything we have, especially those who even fight against the Word of God. Yet Christians have this advantage, that they acknowledge themselves in duty bound to serve God for all these things and to be obedient to him [which the world does not know how to do].

We should, therefore, daily practice this article, impress it on our mind, and remember, in all that we see before us, and in everything good that comes our way, and wherever we escape from calamity or danger, that it is God who gives and does all these things. [From this] we sense and see [God's] paternal heart and his transcendent love toward us. Through this, [our] heart would be warmed and kindled to be thankful and to use all such good things to the honor and praise of God.

Thus we have briefly presented the meaning of this article, as much as is at first necessary for the most simple to learn, both as to what we have and receive from God and what we owe in return, which is a most excellent knowledge but a far greater treasure. For here we see how the Father has given himself to us, together with all creatures, and has most richly provided for us in this life. Indeed, even beyond this, he has overwhelmed us with unspeakable, eternal treasures by his Son and the Holy Spirit, as we shall [later] hear.

11

THE LORD'S PRAYER

In this section of the Large Catechism (1529), Luther discusses the
Lord's Prayer. In the introductory section reproduced below, Luther ar-
ticulates a short theology of prayer for his readers. Luther understood
that prayer is central to the practice of the Christian faith.

Luther argues that prayer is a duty. God commands us to pray. By
giving us the Lord's Prayer, Christ has provided a specific rubric for
our use. For this reason, those who do not call on God cannot ultimately receive his blessings. This is not only because they have been
disobedient by not praying to him as he has commanded but also
because they have not trusted that God will give them what they ask.
If one does not pray, one demonstrates by one's behavior that one
does not trust that God is the gracious God of the gospel who gives
all good things to those who trustingly ask.

From this it also follows that prayer is not only a duty but carries with it God's promise attached to it. God promises to hear and
respond to the prayers of true believers. He promises to bestow all
good things on those who ask him. This also relates to God's gift of
the very words through which we are to address him in the Lord's
Prayer. In the Lord's Prayer we have been given a gracious assurance that the things for which we pray will truly be pleasing to God.

In this, God answers our prayers because he has promised to do so. In no way is his answer to our prayers dependent on our personal worthiness.

Here it would seem that Luther is partially reacting to the medieval Roman Catholic theology of prayer. In the medieval church, it was commonly believed that the prayers of the saints were of greater worth to God than those of ordinary believers. This is because, when compared to ordinary Christians, the saints possessed superior merit, which they had accumulated by performing a greater number of good works.

This notion served as the rationale for the medieval practice of invoking the saints. "Invoking" the saints meant the practice of ordinary Christians reverently speaking to them in heaven. Most Protestants would probably view this practice as constituting prayer to the saints. Nevertheless, it should be emphasized that Roman Catholics generally attempt to distinguish this activity from prayer. In Catholic theology, prayer is directed to God alone. Invocation means asking another who is closer to God in heaven to pray for you. Hence, when ordinary Christians invoked the saints in heaven, the Catholic Church taught that the saints would hear them and then relay the concerns of believers to God by praying on their behalf.

Luther rejects the medieval conception of prayer on these points. Rather, the reformer teaches that prayer (much like creation and redemption) is effective by God's grace alone. Ultimately, our prayers are pleasing to God not because we or the saints are worthy of having them fulfilled. Rather, they are pleasing because he has graciously promised that they are so and that he will hear them. Furthermore, he has also graciously promised to communicate all good things to us if we call on him in prayer.

The last part of this selection deals with the first petition of the Lord's Prayer: "Hallowed be thy name." Luther states here that when we pray that God's name be made holy, we are not praying that it become holy because it is not holy already. God is holy in himself, and consequently his name is already holy as well. Rather, what we are asking for is that God might make his name holy within us.

This raises the question as to what it means for God's name to be holy within believers. Luther answers that because God is a God of grace, he wants to be our supreme object of trust. Therefore God's name is holy in us when we trust in it and therefore call on it in times of need. Likewise, God's name is holy in us when we praise his name for the good things that he has given to us.

Conversely, since Christians are known by God's name (because they have been baptized in the name of the Trinity), when they behave in an ungrateful or immoral manner, they dishonor God's name and it ceases to be holy in them. Therefore, in praying this petition, we not only ask that God may preserve true faith and obedience within us, but also that he might guard us against any behavior that would dishonor his name.

We have now heard what we must do and believe,[1] in which things the best and happiest life consists. Now follows the third part: how we ought to pray. For since we are so constituted that no man can perfectly keep the Ten Commandments, even though he has begun to believe, and since the devil with all his power, together with the world and our own flesh, resists our endeavors, nothing is so necessary as that we should continually resort to the ear of God. [We should] call on him and pray to him that he would give, preserve, and increase in us faith and the fulfillment of the Ten Commandments and that he would remove everything that is in our way and opposes us therein. But that we might know what and how to pray, our Lord Christ has himself taught us both the mode and the words, as we shall see.

But before we explain the Lord's Prayer part by part, it is extremely necessary first to exhort and incite people to prayer, as Christ and the apostles also have done. And the first matter is to know that it is our duty to pray because of God's commandment.

1. Here Luther is referring to the two previous sections of the Large Catechism, which deal with the Ten Commandments and the Apostles' Creed.

For we have heard in the second commandment, "You shall not take the name of the Lord your God in vain,"[2] that we are there required to praise that holy name and call on it in every need, or to pray. For to call on the name of God is nothing else than to pray. Prayer is therefore as strictly and earnestly commanded as all other commandments: to have no other God, not to kill, not to steal, etc. Let no one think that it is all the same whether he prays or does not, as vulgar people do, who grope in such delusion and ask, "Why should I pray? Who knows whether God heeds or will hear my prayer? If I do not pray, someone else will." And thus they fall into the habit of never praying, and on the basis of the claim there is no duty or need of prayer, since we reject false and hypocritical prayers.

But this is true indeed that such prayers as have been offered up until now when men were babbling and bawling in the churches were no [real] prayers. For such external matters, when they are properly observed, may be a good exercise for young children, scholars, and simple persons and may be called singing or reading but not really praying. But praying, as the second commandment teaches, is to call on God in every need. This he requires of us and has not left it to our choice. But it is our duty and obligation to pray if we would be Christians, as much as it is our duty and obligation to obey our parents and the government. For by calling on it and praying, the name of God is honored and profitably used. This you must note above all things, that thereby you may silence and hold back such thoughts as would keep and deter us from prayer. For it would

2. Much like Roman Catholics, Luther and the later Lutheran Church did not view the prohibition against the making of idols as separate from the command not to have any gods before the Lord. Consequently, they number the Ten Commandments differently than the Eastern church and most other Protestants. What most Protestants would consider to be the third commandment Luther refers to as the second.

be improper for a son to say to his father, "Of what use is my obedience? I will go and do what I please, it is all the same." But there stands the commandment: "You shall and must do it, so also here it is not left to my will to do it or leave it undone, but prayer shall and must be offered at the risk of God's wrath and displeasure."

This is therefore to be understood and noted before everything else in order that thereby we may silence and repel the thoughts that would keep and deter us from praying, as though it were not of much consequence if we do not pray or as though it were commanded [to] those who are holier and in better favor with God than we. Indeed, the human heart is by nature so despondent that it always flees from God and imagines that he does not want or desire our prayer because we are sinners and have merited nothing but wrath. Against such thoughts we should regard this commandment and turn to God that we may not by such disobedience provoke his anger all the more. For by this commandment he gives us plainly to understand that he will not cast us from him nor chase us away, although we are sinners, but rather draw us to himself so that we might humble ourselves before him, bewail this misery and plight of ours, and pray for grace and help. Therefore we read in the Scriptures that he is angry also with those who were punished for their sin because they did not return to him and by their prayers assuage his wrath and seek his grace.

Now, from the fact that it is so solemnly commanded to pray, you are to conclude and think that no one should by any means despise his prayer but rather set great store by it and always seek an illustration from the other commandments. A child should by no means despise his obedience to father and mother but should always think, "This work is a work of obedience, and what I do, I do with no other intention than that I may walk in the obedience and commandment of God, on which I can settle and stand firm, and esteem it a great thing, not on account of my worthiness but on account of the commandment." So here also, what and for what we pray we should regard as demanded by God and done in obedience to him and should reflect thus: "On my account it would amount to nothing; but it shall avail because God has commanded it." Therefore everyone, no matter what he has to say in prayer, should always come before God in obedience to this commandment.

We pray, therefore, and exhort everyone most diligently to take this to heart and by no means to despise our prayer. For up to this point it has been taught in this manner in the devil's name that no one regarded these things, and men believed it to be enough to have done the work [of prayer], whether God was to hear it or not. But that is staking prayer on a risk and murmuring it at a venture, and therefore it is a lost prayer. For we allow such thoughts as these to lead us astray and deter us: "I am not holy or worthy enough; if I were as godly and holy as St. Peter or St. Paul, only then I would pray." But put such thoughts far away, for just the same commandment that applied to St. Paul applies also to me. And the second commandment is given as much on my account as on his account, so that he can boast of no better or holier commandment.

Therefore you should say, "My prayer is as precious, holy, and pleasing to God as that of St. Paul or of the most holy saints." This is the reason: "For I will gladly grant that he is holier in his person, but not on account of the commandment, since God does not regard prayer on account of the person but on account of his word and obedience thereto. For on the commandment on which all the saints rest their prayer I, too, rest mine. Moreover, I pray for the same thing for which they all pray and always have prayed. Besides, I have just as great a need of it as those great saints, indeed, even a greater one than they."

Let this be the first and most important point, that all our prayers must be based and rest on obedience to God, irrespective of our person, whether we are sinners or saints, worthy or unworthy. And we must know that God will not treat it like a joke but be angry and punish all who do not pray, as surely as he punishes all other disobedience. Beyond this, he will not suffer our prayers to be in vain or lost. For if he did not intend to answer your prayer, he would not bid you pray and add such a severe commandment to it.

In the second place, we should be the more urged and incited to pray because God has also added a promise and declared that it shall surely be done to us as we pray, as he says [in] Psalm 50:15: "Call upon me in the day of trouble; I will deliver you, and you shall glorify me." And Christ in the Gospel of St. Matthew 7:7–8: "Ask, and it will be given to you. . . . For everyone who asks receives." Such promises ought certainly to encourage and kindle our hearts to pray with pleasure and delight, since he testifies with his [own] word that our prayer is heartily pleasing to him, moreover, that it shall assuredly be heard and granted, in order that we may not despise it or think lightly of it and pray at a venture.

This you can hold up to him and say, "Here I come, dear Father, and pray, not of my own purpose nor upon my own worthiness but on the basis of your commandment and promise, which cannot fail or deceive me." Whoever, therefore, does not believe this promise must know again that he provokes God's anger as a person who most highly dishonors him and accuses him of dishonesty.

Besides this, we should be incited and drawn to prayer because in addition to this commandment and promise God anticipates us, and himself arranges the words and form of prayer for us, and places them on our lips as to how and what we should pray. [He does this in order] that we may see how much he pities us in our distress and may never doubt that such prayer is pleasing to him and shall certainly be answered. [For this reason, the Lord's Prayer] is a great advantage indeed over all other prayers that we might compose ourselves. For in them the conscience would always be in doubt and say, "I have prayed, but who knows whether it pleases him or if I have hit on the right proportions and form?" Hence there is no more noble prayer to be found on earth than the Lord's Prayer, which we daily pray, because it has this excellent testimony that God loves to hear it, which we ought not to surrender for all the riches of the world.

And it has been prescribed also for this reason that we should see and consider the distress that ought to urge and compel us to pray without ceasing. For whoever would pray must have something to present, state, and name that he desires. If not, it cannot be called a prayer.

Therefore we have rightly rejected the prayers of monks and priests, who howl and growl day and night like fiends, [while at the same time] none of them think of praying for a hair's breadth of anything. And if we would assemble all the churches, together with all ecclesiastics,[3] they would be obliged to confess that they have never prayed from their heart even for a drop of wine. For none of them has ever intended to pray from obedience to God and faith in his promise, nor has anyone regarded any distress, but (when they had done their best) they thought no further than this, to do a good work, whereby they might repay God, as being unwilling to take anything from him but wishing only to give him something.

---

3. By "ecclesiastics" Luther means church officials (bishops, priests, etc.) as well as monks, friars, and nuns.

But where there is to be a true prayer, there must be the utmost sincerity. Men must feel their distress, and such distress as presses them and compels them to call and cry out. [By this,] prayer will be made spontaneously, as it ought to be, and men will require no teaching [of] how to prepare for it and to attain to the proper devotion. But the distress that should concern us most, both in regard to ourselves and everyone, you will find abundantly set forth in the Lord's Prayer. Therefore it is to serve also to remind us of the same, that we contemplate it and place it on our heart, lest we become negligent in prayer. For we all have enough that we lack, but the great want is that we do not feel nor see it. Therefore God also requires that you lament and plead such necessities and needs, not because he does not know them but that you may kindle your heart to stronger and greater desires and make wide and open your cloak to receive much.

Therefore, every one of us should accustom himself from his youth daily to pray for all his needs, whenever he is sensible of anything affecting his interests or that of other people among whom he may live, as for preachers, the government, neighbors, domestics, and always (as we have said) to hold up to God his commandment and promise, knowing that he will not have them disregarded. This I say because I would like to see these things brought home again to the people that they might learn to truly pray and not go about coldly and indifferently, whereby they become daily more unfit for prayer, which is just what the devil desires and for what he works with all his powers. For he is well aware what damage and harm it does him when prayer is in proper practice.

For we must know this, that all our shelter and protection rest in prayer alone. For we are far too weak to cope with the devil and all his power and those persons who set themselves against us, and they might easily crush us under their feet. Therefore we must consider and take up those weapons with which Christians must be armed in order to stand against the devil. For what do you think has up to this point accomplished such great things, has checked or quelled the counsels, purposes, murder, and riot of our enemies, whereby the devil intended to crush us, together with the gospel, except that the prayer of a few godly men intervened like a wall of iron on our side? They should else have witnessed a far different tragedy—namely, how the devil would have destroyed all Germany in its own blood. But now they may confidently deride it and make a mockery of it. However, we should nevertheless be a match both for themselves and the devil by prayer alone if we only persevere diligently and not become slack. For whenever a godly Christian prays, "Dear Father, let your will be done," God speaks from on high and says, "Yes, dear child, it shall be so, in spite of the devil and all the world."

Let this be said as an exhortation, that men may learn, first of all, to regard prayer as something great and precious and to make a proper distinction between babbling and praying for something. For we by no means reject prayer, but the bare, useless howling and murmuring we reject, as Christ himself also rejects and prohibits unnecessarily long speeches. Now we shall most briefly and clearly treat of the Lord's Prayer. Here there is comprehended in seven successive articles, or petitions, every need that never ceases to relate to us, and each so great that it ought to constrain us to keep praying it all our lives.

The First Petition

Hallowed be Thy name.

This is, indeed, somewhat obscure and not expressed in good German, for in our mother tongue we would say, "Heavenly Father, help that by all means your name may be holy." But what is it to pray that his name may be holy? Is it not holy already? Answer: Yes, it is always holy by its very nature, but our use of it is not holy. For God's name was given us when we became Christians and were baptized, so that we are called children of God and have the sacraments, by which he so incorporates us into himself that everything that is God's must serve for our use.

Here now the great need exists for which we ought to be most concerned, that this name have its proper honor and be esteemed holy and sublime as the greatest treasure and sanctuary that we have, and that as godly children we pray that the name of God, which is already holy in heaven, may also be and remain holy with us on earth and in all the world.

But how does [the name of God] become holy among us? The plainest answer can be given as [this]: When both our doctrine and life are godly and Christian. For since in this prayer we call God our Father, it is our duty always to conduct ourselves as godly children, that he may receive not shame but honor and praise from us.

Now the name of God is profaned by us either in words or deed. (For whatever we do on the earth must be either words or deeds, speech or act.) In the first place, then, it is profaned when men preach, teach, and speak in the name of God what is false and misleading so that his name serves as a means to adorn and to make acceptable their falsehood. Indeed, that is the greatest profanation and dishonor of the divine name. Furthermore, [the name of God is profaned] also when men, by swearing, cursing, conjuring, etc., grossly abuse the holy name as a covering for their shame.

In the second place, [it is profaned] also by an openly wicked life and works, when those who are called Christians and the people of God are adulterers, drunkards, misers, envious, and slanderers. Here again must the name of God come to shame and be profaned because of us. For just as it is a shame and disgrace to a natural father to have a bad, perverse child that opposes him in words and deeds, in that he suffers contempt and reproach because of it, so also it brings dishonor on God if we who are called by his name and have all manner of goods from him teach, speak, and live in any other manner except as godly and heavenly children so that people say of us that we must be not God's but the devil's children.

Thus you see that in this petition we pray just for that which God demands in the second commandment—namely, that his name be not taken in vain to swear, curse, lie, deceive, etc., but be usefully employed to the praise and honor of God. For whoever employs the name of God for any sort of wrong profanes and desecrates this holy name, as in previous times a church was considered desecrated when a murder or any other crime had been committed in it, or when a pyx[4] or relic was desecrated, as being holy in themselves yet becoming unholy in use. Thus this point is easy and clear if only the language is understood, that to hallow is the same as in our idiom to praise, magnify, and honor both in word and deed.

Here now, learn how great a need there is of such prayer. For because we see how full the world is of sects and false teachers, who all wear the holy name as a cover and sham for their doctrines of devils, we ought by all means to pray without ceasing and to cry and call on God against all such as preach and believe falsely and whatever opposes and persecutes our gospel and pure doctrine and would suppress it, as bishops, tyrants, enthusiasts,[5]

4. This refers to a small box used to hold a consecrated Eucharistic wafer. In Orthodox, Catholic, and Anglican churches, these boxes are used to carry communion wafers to sick persons unable to attend a Sunday service.

5. By "enthusiast" Luther means different Christian sects in the sixteenth century who ignored the Bible and instead sought the Spirit through their own inner feelings and sense of the truth. These groups often had ministries that centered on people who claimed to

etc. Likewise [we ought to pray] also for ourselves who have the Word of God but are not thankful for it, nor live as we ought according to the same. If now you pray for this with your heart, you can be sure that it pleases God. For there is nothing that he would rather hear more than that his honor and praise is exalted above everything else and that his Word is taught in its purity and treated as precious and dear.

---

be prophets on the basis of the inspiration of the Holy Spirit. According to Luther, the papacy would also be an example of this, since the pope claims a form of divine inspiration.

12

THE FIRST COMMANDMENT

In this section of the Large Catechism (1529), Luther discusses the first commandment. Much like his treatment of the Lord's Prayer, Luther views the first commandment as one of both law and grace. The first commandment is law to be obeyed by Christians. Positively, this means that it is the duty of Christians to recognize that God alone is the true God. Negatively, this means that Christians are to flee from all idolatry.

Idolatry is not merely the worship of images, although this is one form that idolatry might take. Rather, idolatry is primarily a matter of the heart. Humans are trusting creatures by nature. Things we trust in above all else serve as a kind of central principle by which we guide our lives. In this manner, the essence of the whole law can be found in the first commandment. In obeying God, we show that we trust that the law is his will and that it has been given to us for our benefit. Therefore, faith and obedience are not opposed to each other but are rather two sides of the same coin. God is worthy of our trust because he is a God of grace. He graciously promises to be our God and work all things for our good in the first commandment: "I am the LORD your God."

Nevertheless, because humans are fallen, they inevitably trust in things that are not the true God. Specifically, humans trust in themselves and other created things. Creaturely idols often include power, sex, beauty, or money. Of course, all these things are not bad in and of themselves. Rather, they are manifestations of God's love and care for us as his creatures. Nonetheless, these good things become a problem when humans cease to believe God's Word that he is the source of everything good and therefore should be trusted above all things. Rejecting God's Word, fallen humans inevitably trust in wealth, sex, beauty, power, and other created things as ultimate sources of the good. This is what it means to make God's gifts into idols.

Luther goes on to give many examples of idolatry in his own day. First, the reformer speaks of the medieval cult of the saints. Luther implicitly suggests that the distinction Roman Catholics make between veneration (which is honor and trust given in a less than ultimate sense to the saints) and worship (honor and trust offered up in an ultimate sense to God) is irrelevant. From the reformer's perspective, since true worship is constituted by proper trust, then medieval Christians effectively worshiped the saints by trusting in them above God. Instead of God's name, medieval people called on the saints in a time of trouble or crisis. As a result, they attributed the good things they received to the saints rather than God alone.

Second, Luther uses an example that is still very relevant in our own day—namely, the worship of money. People assume that if they have enough money, they have effectively returned to the garden of Eden. Those who do not have money feel that their lives are miserable and that God does not care about them. This suggests that people are more apt to trust in money than in God. Nevertheless, people with money in this life must lose it in the end. They will die, and their money will be of no use to them. Moreover, it is fairly likely that those to whom they left their money will squander it after they are gone. Indeed, families rarely stay wealthy beyond a few generations. Conversely, God gives gifts that are imperishable. He will give those who trust in him eternal life in which there will be no need for money.

Ultimately, the true God reveals himself to be the only object worthy of our trust. When tested, he is the only god who does not fail. For this reason, we should fear and love him in faith. Christians fear God when they flee from those things that God has commanded them to avoid and repent when they disobey him. Likewise, believers love God when they repent and trust in God as the sole author of all that is good, most especially their salvation in Christ. Through this trust, they are empowered to obey his commandments and praise God as the sole Author of all good things.

You will have no other gods before me.

That is: "You shall have [and worship] me alone as your God." What is the force of this, and how is it to be understood? What does it mean to have a god? Or, what is God? Answer: A god means that from which we are to expect all good and to which we are to take refuge in all distress, so that to have a god is nothing else than to trust and believe him from the [whole] heart. As I have often said, the confidence and faith of the heart alone make both God and an idol. If your faith and trust be right, then is your God also true. And, on the other hand, if your trust is false and wrong, then you do not have the true God. For these two belong together, faith and God. I say that the thing on which you set your heart and put your trust is properly your god.

Therefore it is the intent of this commandment to require true faith and trust of the heart that settles on the only true God and clings to him alone. That is as much as to say, "See to it that you let me alone be your God and never seek another"—i.e., "Whatever you lack of good things, expect it of me and look to me for it, and whenever you suffer misfortune and distress, creep and cling to me. I, yes, I, will give you enough and help you out of every need. Only do not let your heart cling to or rest on anything else."

This I must unfold somewhat more plainly, that it may be understood and perceived by ordinary examples of the contrary.

Many think that he has God and everything in abundance when he has money and possessions. He trusts in them and boasts of them with such firmness and assurance as to care for no one. Indeed, such a man also has a god, Mammon by name—i.e., money and possessions—on which he sets all his heart and which is also the most common idol on earth. He who has money and possessions feels secure and is joyful and undismayed as though he were sitting in the midst of Paradise. On the other hand, he who has none doubts and is despondent, as though he knew of no God. For very few are to be found who are cheerful and who neither mourn nor complain if they do not have Mammon. This [care and desire for money] sticks and clings to our nature, even to the grave.

So, too, whoever trusts and boasts that he possesses great skill, prudence, power, favor, friendship, and honor has also a god, but not this true and only God. This appears again when you notice how presumptuous, secure, and proud people are because of such possessions and how despondent when they no longer exist or are withdrawn. Therefore I repeat that the chief explanation of this point is that to have a god is to have something in which the heart entirely trusts.

Besides, consider what, in our blindness, we have up to now been practicing and doing under the papacy. If anyone had a toothache, he fasted and honored St. Apollonia. If he was afraid of fire, he chose St. Lawrence as his helper in need. If he dreaded pestilence, he made a vow to St. Sebastian or Rochio. [Indeed, there were] a countless number of such abominations, where everyone selected his own saint, worshiped him, and called for help to him in distress.[1] Here belong those also—as, e.g., sorcer-

---

1. Luther is here referring to the Roman Catholic practice of calling upon and paying adoration to the saints. In the Roman Catholic conception, people on earth can call upon saints in heaven to pray for them and intercede for them, in the same way that one asks

ers and magicians—whose idolatry is gross in the extreme and who make a covenant with the devil in order that he may give them plenty of money or help them in love affairs, preserve their cattle, restore to them lost possessions, etc. For all these place their heart and trust elsewhere than in the true God, look for nothing good to him nor seek it from him.

Thus you can easily understand what and how much this commandment requires—namely, that man's entire heart and all his confidence be placed in God alone and in no one else. For to have God, you can easily perceive, is not to lay hold of him with our hands or to put him in a bag [as you would money] or to lock him in a chest [as you would silver vessels]. But to apprehend him means when the heart lays hold of him and clings to him. But to cling to him with the heart is nothing else than to trust in him entirely. For this reason he wishes to turn us away from everything else that exists outside of him and to draw us to himself—namely, because he is the only eternal good, as though he would say, "Whatever you have up to this time sought from the saints, or for whatever [things] you have trusted in Mammon or anything else, expect it all of me, and regard me as the one who will help you and pour out on you richly all good things."

Indeed, here you have the meaning of the true honor and worship of God, which pleases God and which he commands under penalty of eternal wrath—namely, that the heart knows no other comfort or confidence than in him and does not suffer itself to be torn from him but, for him, risks and disregards everything on earth. On the other hand, you can easily see and

---

another to pray for them here on earth. Since the saints have more merit than ordinary Christians, their prayers are more effective, and the person who invokes them is therefore more likely to get what they desire. Luther also refers to the fact that different saints specialize in different troubles that people might have.

judge how the world practices only false worship and idolatry. For no people has ever been so wicked as not to institute and observe some divine worship. Everyone has set up as his special god whatever he looked to for blessings, help, and comfort.

Thus, for example, the heathen who put their trust in power and dominion elevated Jupiter as the supreme god. The others, who were bent on riches, happiness, or pleasure, and a life of ease, Hercules, Mercury, Venus, or others. Women with child [trusted in] Diana or Lucina, and so on. Thus everyone made his god that which his heart was inclined [toward], so that even in the mind of the heathen to have a god means to trust and believe.[2] But their error is this, that their trust is false and wrong; for it is not placed in the only God, besides whom there is truly no God in heaven or on earth. Therefore the heathen really make their self-invented notions and dreams of God an idol and put their trust in that which is altogether nothing.

Thus it is with all idolatry. For it consists not merely in erecting an image and worshiping it but rather in the heart, which stands gaping at something else and seeks help and consolation from creatures, saints, or devils and neither cares for God nor looks to him for so much good as to believe that he is willing to help, neither believes that whatever good it experiences comes from God.

Besides, there is also a false worship and extreme idolatry that we have up to this point practiced and is still prevalent in the world, on which also all ecclesiastical orders are founded[3] and which concerns the conscience alone, that seeks in its own works help, consolation, and salvation; presumes to wrest heaven from

2. Luther is referring here to the gods of ancient Rome.
3. Luther is here referring to the different orders of monks, friars, and nuns that arose during the Middle Ages, such as the Franciscans, Dominicans, Augustinians, and Benedictines.

God; and reckons how many bequests it has made, how often
it has fasted, celebrated Mass, etc. On such things it depends
and of them boasts, as though unwilling to receive anything
from God as a gift, but desires itself to earn or merit it super-
abundantly, just as though he must serve us and were our debtor
and we his liege lords.[4] What is this but reducing God to an
idol, indeed, [a fig image or] an apple-god,[5] and elevating and
regarding ourselves as God? But this is slightly too subtle and
is not for young pupils.

But let this be said to the simple, that they may well note and
remember the meaning of this commandment—namely, that
we are to trust in God alone and look to him and expect from
him nothing but good, as from one who gives us body, life, food,
drink, nourishment, health, protection, peace, and all necessaries
of both temporal and eternal things. He also preserves us from
misfortune and, if any evil happens to us, delivers and rescues us,
so that it is God alone (as has been sufficiently said) from whom
we receive all good and by whom we are delivered from all evil.
Hence also, I think, we Germans from ancient times call God
(more elegantly and appropriately than any other language) by
that name from the word "good," as being an eternal fountain
that gushes forth abundantly nothing but what is good and from
which flows forth all that is and is called "good."[6]

For even though otherwise we experience much good from
men, still whatever we receive by his command or arrangement

4. In medieval society, a liege lord was a person who ruled a particular territory in
the name of a king. The king would give him a title, land, and serfs to work the land, and
in exchange, he would obey the king and usually follow the king into war, if necessary.

5. By "fig image" or "apple-god" Luther means a pagan deity who can be controlled
through our actions.

6. Luther is claiming that the German word "Gott" (God) is etymologically based
on the German word "Gut" (Good). Although Luther displays many fine theological
insights here, his etymology is not at all correct.

is all received from God. For our parents, and all rulers, and everyone besides with respect to his neighbor, have received from God the command that they should do us all manner of good so that we receive these blessings not from them but, through them, from God. For creatures are only the hands, channels, and means whereby God gives all things, as he gives to the mother breasts and milk to offer to her child and corn and all manner of produce from the earth for nourishment, none of which blessings could be produced by any creature of itself.

Therefore no man should presume to take or give anything except as God has commanded, in order that it may be acknowledged as God's gift and thanks may be rendered him for it, as this commandment requires. On this account also these means of receiving good gifts through creatures are not to be rejected, neither should we in presumption seek other ways and means than God has commanded. For that would not be receiving from God but seeking of ourselves.

Let everyone, then, see to it that he regards this commandment great and high above all things, and do not think of it as a joke. Ask and examine your heart diligently, and you will find whether it cleaves to God alone or not. If you have a heart that can expect of him nothing but what is good, especially in want and distress, and that, moreover, renounces and forsakes everything that is not God, then you have the only true God. If, on the contrary, it cleaves to anything else, of which it expects a greater good and help than of God, and does not take refuge in him but in adversity flees from him, then you have an idol, another god. In order that it may be seen that God will not have this commandment thrown to the winds but will most strictly enforce it, he has attached to it first a terrible threat and then a beautiful, comforting promise that is also to be urged and impressed on young people, that they may take it to heart and retain it: "For I the LORD your God am a jealous God, visiting the iniquity of the fathers on the children to the third and fourth generation of those who hate me, but showing steadfast love to thousands of those who love me and keep my commandments" [Exod. 20:5–6].

Although these words relate to all the commandments (as we shall hereafter learn), yet they are joined to this chief commandment because it is of first importance that men have a right head. For where the head is right, the whole life must be right, and vice versa. Learn, therefore, from these words how angry God is with those who trust in anything but him and, again, how good and gracious he is to those who trust and believe in him alone with the whole heart, so that his anger does not cease until the fourth generation while, on the other hand, his blessing and goodness extend to many thousands, lest you live in such security and commit yourself to chance as men of brutal heart who think that it makes no great difference [how they live]. He is a God who will not leave it unavenged if men turn from him, and will not stop being angry until the fourth generation, even until they are utterly exterminated. Therefore he is to be feared and not to be despised.

He has also demonstrated this in all history, as the Scriptures abundantly show and daily experience still teaches. For from the beginning he has utterly destroyed all idolatry and, on account of it, both heathen and Jews, even as at the present day he overthrows all false worship, so that all who remain therein must finally perish. Therefore, although proud, powerful, and rich worldly people are now to be found who boast defiantly of their Mammon with utter disregard whether God is angry at or smiles on them and dare to withstand his wrath, yet they will not succeed; but before they are aware, they shall be wrecked, along with all in which they trusted. [Similarly], all others have perished who have thought themselves more secure or powerful.

And just because of such hardened heads who imagine that because God connives and allows them to rest in security he either is entirely ignorant or cares nothing about such matters, he must deal a smashing blow and punish them, so that he cannot forget it unto children's children, so that everyone may take note and see that this is no joke to him. For they are those whom he refers to when he says, "Those who hate me" (i.e., those who persist in their defiance and pride). [Indeed], whatever is preached or said to them, they will not listen. When they are reproved, in order that they may learn to know themselves and change their ways before the punishment begins, they become mad and foolish so as to fairly earn wrath, as we now see daily in bishops and princes.

But terrible as are these threats, so much the more powerful is the consolation in the promise that those who cling to God alone should be sure that he will show them mercy. That is to say, [God will] show them pure goodness and blessing, not only for themselves but also to their children and children's children, even to the thousandth generation and beyond that. This ought certainly to move and impel us to fix our hearts in all confidence on God if we wish all temporal and eternal good, since the Supreme Majesty makes such sublime offers and presents such cordial invitations and such rich promises.

Therefore, everyone should take this seriously to heart, unless it be regarded as though a man had spoken it. For to you it is a question either of eternal blessing, happiness, and salvation or of eternal wrath, misery, and woe. What more would you have or desire than that he so kindly promises to be yours with every blessing and to protect and help you in all need? But, alas, here is the failure, that the world does not believe any of this. Neither does it have any regard for God's Word, because it sees that those who trust in God and not in Mammon suffer care and want and the devil opposes and resists them, that they have neither money, favor, nor honor, and besides can scarcely support life. On the other hand, those who serve Mammon have power, favor, honor, possessions, and every comfort in the eyes of the world. For this reason, these words must be grasped as being directed against such appearances, and we must consider that they do not lie or deceive but must come true.

Reflect for yourself or investigate and tell me: Those who have used all their care and diligence to accumulate great possessions and wealth, what have they finally attained? You will find that they have wasted their toil and labor, or even though they have amassed great treasures, they have been dispersed and scattered, so that they themselves have never found happiness in their wealth and afterward it never reached the third generation.

Indeed, you will find plenty of instances of this in all histories, also in the memory of elderly and experienced people. Just observe and think about them. Saul was a great king, chosen of God, and a godly man. But when he was established on his throne and let his heart decline from God and put his trust in his crown and power, he was destroyed with everything that he had, so that none even of his children remained.

David, on the other hand, was a poor, despised man, hunted down and chased, so that he nowhere felt secure of his life. Yet he remained in spite of Saul and became king. For these words had to remain and come true, since God cannot lie or deceive. Only let not the devil and the world deceive you with their show, which indeed remains for a time but finally is nothing.

Let us, then, learn the first commandment well, that we may see how God will not tolerate presumption nor trust in any other object and how he requires nothing higher of us than confidence from the heart for everything good. [From this starting point], we may proceed right and straightforward and use all the blessings that God gives no further than as a shoemaker uses his needle, awl, and thread for work and then lays them aside, or as a traveler uses an inn and food and his bed only for temporal necessity, each one in his station, according to God's order, and without allowing any of these things to be our lord or idol. Let this suffice with respect to the first commandment, which we have had to explain at length, since it is of chief importance, because, as before said, where the heart is rightly disposed toward God and this commandment is observed, all the others follow.

A Note about Sources

The texts of Luther's writings are based on the following translations. The texts have been updated by Jack D. Kilcrease, in
consultation with the German originals, to reflect modern usage.
Scripture quotations have been conformed to the ESV.

The selection from *On Christian Liberty* is based on the translation by Henry Wace and C. A. Buchheim, from the book *First
Principles of the Reformation* (London: John Murray, 1883).

The selections from *Commentary on Galatians* are based on
the translation in *Commentary on the Epistle to the Galatians*
(1531), trans. and abridged by Theodore Graebner (Grand
Rapids: Zondervan, 1949), 105–13, 113–18.

The text of *Preface to St. Paul's Letter to the Romans* is based
on the translation by Brother Andrew Thornton, OSB, for the
Saint Anselm College Humanities Program, © 1983 by Saint
Anselm Abbey, accessed September 13, 2015, http://www.ccel
.org/l/luther/romans/pref_romans.html.

The selections from the Large Catechism are based on the
translation in *Concordia Triglotta: The Symbolic Books of the*

Evangelical Lutheran Church, trans. W. H. T. Dau and F. Bente (St. Louis: Concordia, 1921), 581–93, 679–83, 683–87, 687–97, 697–711.

The text of *That Doctrines of Men Are to Be Rejected* is based on the translation in *Works of Martin Luther*, trans. William Lambert (Philadelphia: Castle Press, 1915), 431–55.

The text of *The Bondage of the Will* is based on the translation by Edward Thomas Vaughan (London: J. and T. Combe, 1823), 17–22.

The text of *True and False Views of Christ's Suffering* is based on *The Precious and Sacred Writings of Martin Luther*, vol. 11, trans. John Lenker (Minneapolis: Lutherans in All Lands Press, 1906), 183–92.

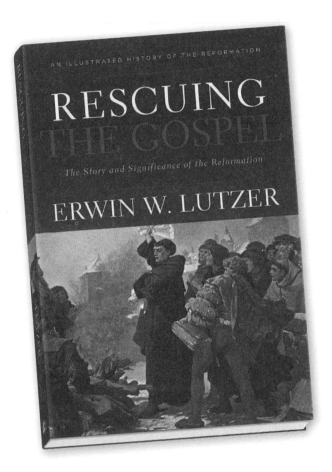